THE WAY
PEOPLE
LIVE

Life in Ancient China

Titles in The Way People Live series include:

Cowboys in the Old West
Games of Ancient Rome
Life Among the Great Plains
  Indians
Life Among the Ibo Women of
  Nigeria
Life Among the Indian Fighters
Life Among the Pirates
Life Among the Samurai
Life Among the Vikings
Life During the Black Death
Life During the Crusades
Life During the French
  Revolution
Life During the Gold Rush
Life During the Great
  Depression
Life During the Middle Ages
Life During the Renaissance
Life During the Russian
  Revolution
Life During the Spanish
  Inquisition
Life in a Japanese American
  Internment Camp
Life in a Medieval Castle
Life in a Medieval Monastery
Life in a Nazi Concentration
  Camp
Life in Ancient Athens
Life in Ancient Greece
Life in Ancient Rome
Life in a Wild West Show
Life in Charles Dickens's
  England

Life in the Amazon Rain Forest
Life in the American Colonies
Life in Ancient China
Life in Ancient Egypt
Life in Communist Russia
Life in the Elizabethan Theater
Life in Genghis Khan's Mongolia
Life in the Hitler Youth
Life in Moscow
Life in the North During the
  Civil War
Life in the South During the
  Civil War
Life in Tokyo
Life in the Warsaw Ghetto
Life in War-Torn Bosnia
Life of a Medieval Knight
Life of a Nazi Soldier
Life of a Roman Slave
Life of a Roman Soldier
Life of a Slave on a Southern
  Plantation
Life on Alcatraz
Life on a Medieval Pilgrimage
Life on an African Slave Ship
Life on an Everest Expedition
Life on Ellis Island
Life on the American Frontier
Life on the Oregon Trail
Life on the Underground
  Railroad
Life Under the Jim Crow Laws

THE WAY
PEOPLE
LIVE

Life in Ancient China

by Amy Allison

Lucent Books, P.O. Box 289011, San Diego, CA 92198-9011

Library of Congress Cataloging-in-Publication Data

Allison, Amy, 1956–
    Life in ancient China / by Amy Allison.
        p.   cm. — (The way people live)
    Includes bibliographical references and index.
    Summary: Discusses life in China primarily during the Han dynasty,
describing the life of farmers, life in a city, life in the military, business
practices, the arts, and more.
    ISBN 1-56006-694-6 (lib. : alk. paper)
    1. China—Civilization—221 B.C.–960 A.D.—Juvenile literature.
    2. China—Social life and customs—221 B.C.–960 A.D.—Juvenile literature.
    [1. China—Civilization—221 B.C.–960 A.D. 2. China—Social life and
customs—221 B.C.–960 A.D.] I. Title.   II. Series.
    DS747.42.A45   2001
    931'.04—dc21   00–008752

Contents

Discovering the Humanity in Us All

Books in The Way People Live series focus on groups of people in a wide variety of circumstances, settings, and time periods. Some books focus on different cultural groups, others, on people in a particular historical time period, while others cover people involved in a specific event. Each book emphasizes the daily routines, personal and historical struggles, and achievements of people from all walks of life.

To really understand any culture, it is necessary to strip the mind of the common notions we hold about groups of people. These stereotypes are the archenemies of learning. It does not even matter whether the stereotypes are positive or negative; they are confining and tight. Removing them is a challenge that's not easily met, as anyone who has ever tried it will admit. Ideas that do not fit into the templates we create are unwelcome visitors—ones we would prefer remain quietly in a corner or forgotten room.

The cowboy of the Old West is a good example of such confining roles. The cowboy was courageous, yet soft-spoken. His time (it is always a he, in our template) was spent alternatively saving a rancher's daughter from certain death on a runaway stagecoach, or shooting it out with rustlers. At times, of course, he was likely to get a little crazy in town after a trail drive, but for the most part, he was the epitome of inner strength. It is disconcerting to find out that the cowboy is human, even a bit childish. Can it really be true that cowboys would line up to help the

cook on the trail drive grind coffee, just hoping he would give them a little stick of peppermint candy that came with the coffee shipment? The idea of tough cowboys vying with one another to help "Coosie" (as they called their cooks) for a bit of candy seems silly and out of place.

So is the vision of Eskimos playing video games and watching MTV, living in prefab housing in the Arctic. It just does not fit with what "Eskimo" means. We are far more comfortable with snow igloos and whale blubber, harpoons and kayaks.

Although the cultures dealt with in Lucent's The Way People Live series are often historically and socially well known, the emphasis is on the personal aspects of life. Groups of people, while unquestionably affected by their politics and their governmental structures, are more than those institutions. How do people in a particular time and place educate their children? What do they eat? And how do they build their houses? What kinds of work do they do? What kinds of games do they enjoy? The answers to these questions bring these cultures to life. People's lives are revealed in the particulars and only by knowing the particulars can we understand these cultures' will to survive and their moments of weakness and greatness.

This is not to say that understanding politics does not help to understand a culture. There is no question that the Warsaw ghetto, for example, was a culture that was brought about by the politics and social ideas of Adolf

Hitler and the Third Reich. But the Jews who were crowded together in the ghetto cannot be understood by the Reich's politics. Their life was a day-to-day battle for existence, and the creativity and methods they used to prolong their lives is a vital story of human perseverance that would be denied by focusing only on the institutions of Hitler's Germany. Knowing that children as young as five or six outwitted Nazi guards on a daily basis, that Jewish policemen helped the Germans control the ghetto, that children attended secret schools in the ghetto and even earned diplomas—these are the things that reveal the fabric of life, that can inspire, intrigue, and amaze.

Books in The Way People Live series allow both the casual reader and the student to see humans as victims, heroes, and onlookers. And although humans act in ways that can fill us with feelings of sorrow and revulsion, it is important to remember that "hero," "predator," and "victim" are dangerous terms. Heaping undue pity or praise on people reduces them to objects, and strips them of their humanity.

Seeing the Jews of Warsaw only as victims is to deny their humanity. Seeing them only as they appear in surviving photos, staring at the camera with infinite sadness, is limiting, both to them and to those who want to understand them. To an object of pity, the only appropriate response becomes "Those poor creatures!" and that reduces both the quality of their struggle and the depth of their despair. No one is served by such two-dimensional views of people and their cultures.

With this in mind, The Way People Live series strives to flesh out the traditional, two-dimensional views of people in various cultures and historical circumstances. Using a wide variety of primary quotations—the words not only of the politicians and government leaders, but of the real people whose lives are being examined—each book in the series attempts to show an honest and complete picture of a culture removed from our own by time or space.

By examining cultures in this way, the reader will notice not only the glaring differences from his or her own culture, but also will be struck by the similarities. For indeed, people share common needs—warmth, good company, stability, and affirmation from others. Ultimately, seeing how people really live, or have lived, can only enrich our understanding of ourselves.

A Balancing Act

Researchers believe that China's civilization began in north-central Asia, in the valley along the Huang He, or Yellow River, probably about 2000 B.C. It was an uncertain beginning. The Huang He would regularly overflow its banks, causing devastating floods. Monsoon storm clouds moving inland from the Indian Ocean would also lose much of their rain before reaching the farmers' fields, causing crops to die for lack of water. As they struggled for survival between extremes of flooding and drought, the people of the Huang He valley came to appreciate the delicate balance of nature.

Not surprisingly in the face of such extremes, the desire for stability pervaded the Chinese way of life. In later centuries, that desire underlay the philosophy of social harmony taught by the moral teacher Confucius and his followers. It motivated the myriad rituals, social and religious, that people engaged in daily as well as seasonally.

A traditional-style Chinese pavilion stands along the shore of the Yellow River, where it is believed that China's civilization began around 2000 BC.

The quest for stability also prompted the heavy-handed political control practiced by successive emperors through a massive network of bureaucrats. That bureaucracy was successful in providing some stability. In fact, it was China's civil service that provided continuity in government through changes in imperial dynasties over thousands of years.

The Rise of Qin

Despite cultural similarities across a vast region, China as a unified nation did not exist until 221 B.C. The fall of one dynasty and the rise of the next would be accompanied by civil war. In particular, the fall of the Zhou dynasty in 481 B.C. resulted in such violence that the centuries following were known as the Warring States Period. Lacking a strong central government to rein in their ambitions, feudal lord fought feudal lord, plunging the land into constant warfare.

The common people's longing for peace and stability grew desperate during these times. Armies seized peasant farmers' sons for soldiers and their crops for food. In their lust for victory, military commanders did not hesitate to breach dikes, drowning not only enemy troops but also civilians. Smaller territories were taken over by larger ones that could command more troops as well as more deadly weapons.

By the third century B.C., the state with the mightiest war machine proved to be Qin. Under its ruler, Qin Shihuang, it overran one state after another, "like a silkworm devours a mulberry leaf,"[1] wrote a Chinese historian from a later period. With all of China now under his thumb, Qin Shihuang set about imposing on his new subjects the political philosophy that had won his home state its brutal victories. Known as legalism, this phi-

losophy considered the state, or machinery of government, the ultimate good, so that any action that benefited the state was justified. According to legalism, a supreme, absolute ruler and harsh, far-reaching laws applied without mercy were required to keep the state strong.

Taxes were also required to maintain the government's strength. Grain, used for payment of taxes, had to be weighed and the weight had to be recorded; for taxes due in cash, coins had to be counted. However, differences from region to region in money, measurement, and writing systems made tax collection difficult. To overcome this problem, Qin Shihuang standardized weights and measures, currency, and writing styles throughout the land. In addition, he ordered a standard width for carts along the roads he decreed should be built to link his new empire.

Writing of the emperor's reign, one scholar wrote of Qin Shihuang that "he cracked his great whip to bend the world to his will."[2] He imposed an alarmingly detailed code of law upon his people. The ordinary person was at a loss to be familiar with all of its intricacies. Breaking the law might happen more out of ignorance than intent, though to the emperor's way of thinking, that did not constitute an excuse. Under his regime, an entire family faced punishment for a crime committed by one of its members. And punishments, including amputation of a nose or foot, were not easily avoided.

The mix of harsh laws and burdensome taxes eventually sparked a popular revolt. Soldiers mutinied and peasants took up arms against the state, and after less than twenty years, the Qin dynasty came crashing down. It was replaced by what many historians consider to represent the height of ancient Chinese civilization: the Han dynasty.

The founder of the new dynasty, known to history as Gaozu, or "Great Ancestor,"

A painting depicts the heavy-handed rule of Emperor Qin Shihuang, seen here ordering his men to burn books and execute scholars.

came from peasant stock. One story about Gaozu meeting with a group of scholars conveys his rough-around-the-edges manner: "After listening to their arguments, he expressed his own opinion. Seizing the high official cap of their spokesman, he stood before them and urinated in it."[3]

Despite Gaozu's lack of learning and refinement, he recognized the need for an educated corps of workers to see to the administration of his empire. In fact, the Han dynasty continued and even extended the bureaucratic government system put in place by Qin Shihuang. Nevertheless, the philosophy of rule markedly changed under the Han. Held in contempt and harassed during the reign of Qin Shihuang, scholars steeped in

Confucianism now guided the training of officials running the government. The civilizing impulse of Confucianism, with its emphasis on courteous and deferential behavior, went about achieving a well-ordered society in a more humane way than the rigid authoritarianism dictated by legalism. And that may have made all the difference. The Han dynasty lasted over four hundred years—as opposed to the Qin's fifteen. So thoroughly did the Han dynasty's rule place its stamp on China's culture that more than two thousand years later, the overwhelmingly dominant ethnic group in China is known as the Han. Given the influence of the Han dynasty, it is appropriate to focus on the four-hundred-odd years of Han rule in examining life in ancient China.

1 On the Land

Wresting farmland from the brush and taming floodwaters with dikes and canals proved such daunting tasks that the ancient Chinese attributed the accomplishment of them to mythic heroes. For example, according to tradition, Shen-nong, with an ox's head and a man's body, supposedly taught people to make plows and till the soil. Yu, the legendary "Great Engineer," was believed to have irrigated the fields and curtailed flooding with his water-control works.

Development of irrigation and flood control, along with advances in farming tools and techniques, increased crop yields and supported China's developing civilization. By the time of the Han dynasty, nearly two-thirds of China's people were wresting produce from the soil.

China's emperors took note of farmers' contributions. In 141 B.C. an imperial edict was issued recognizing the nation's dependence on its farmers. The document stated, "Agriculture is the foundation of the empire. As for gold, pearls, and jade, they cannot be eaten in time of hunger, and cannot be worn in time of cold."[4]

The Family Farm

Thanks to this imperial recognition, farming was considered honorable work in ancient China. For example, because peasant farmers—the *nong*—were believed to contribute more to society, they could claim a social and legal

Chinese farm workers toil in the rice fields. Farming was recognized as a vital and honorable profession in ancient China.

status superior to that of artisans and merchants. However, as observed by a first-century B.C. adviser to the emperor, their status meant little in reality: "Now, the law despises merchants, but the merchants have become rich and noble; it esteems peasants, but the peasants have become poor and [lowly]."[5] The *nong* and their families were compelled to dwell in drafty dirt-floor huts, sharing a single room. Under such conditions, life was a constant struggle. Despite their growing of food for the nation, China's farmers themselves sometimes went hungry. "My wife and children did not have enough husks [of grain] and beans to eat and their coarse clothing was not in good condition,"[6] lamented one farmer.

Food was not the only necessity that farmers had to produce for themselves. The loose clothing and sandals worn by the *nong* were made of a rough fabric woven from fibers of

Cultivating Rice

At the dawn of the Han dynasty, rice was a luxury food in parts of China and was believed to possess healing powers. Most people in the north ate wheat and millet, though from the Yangtze Valley southward, rice formed a staple in the diet. Farmers in the southern regions initiated rice cultivation in paddies, or water-immersed fields.

The flow of water into the paddies was carefully controlled to maintain an even depth and temperature. Opening up gaps in mud banks surrounding the paddies caused water to stream into them; by regulating the speed that the water flowed through the paddies, farmers found they could regulate its temperature. Gaps opposite each other caused the water to flow in a relatively short course, keeping it warm, while diagonal gaps lengthened the course and cooled the water.

By the first century B.C., rice was introduced from the warmer, wetter south into north-central China. Innovation was required to grow rice there, with its shorter growing season and relatively dry climate. The crop was first planted and cultivated in nursery seedbeds blanketed with liquid manure. Once the shoots grew to about five inches high, they were transplanted to plowed and fertilized paddy fields.

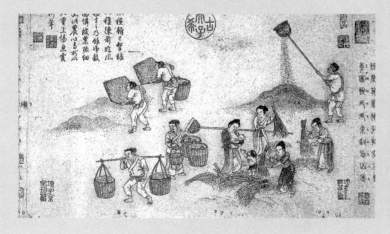

The ancient Chinese became skilled at the harvesting of rice, which during the Han dynasty was just beginning to become a staple food.

the hemp plant, and wool from sheep the farmer raised served as padding between layers of fabric, providing protection from the wind and cold of winter in the northern regions. To shade themselves from the sun, farmers wore hats of either bamboo leaves or rice straw. Rice straw was also crafted into rain-resistant capes.

Producing the clothing the family wore was women's work. "Man as tiller, woman as weaver"[7] is an ancient Chinese saying. Such division of labor did not exempt women from work in the fields, however. Each member of the household, which during the Han period consisted of a husband and wife and two or three children, was assigned farming chores. While for the most part the men plowed and harvested crops, women and children often labored at fertilizing the soil as well as at weeding the cultivated fields.

Children also tended the livestock, which primarily consisted of small animals that were relatively easy to care for, including dogs, pigs, chickens, ducks, and sheep. The meat from such animals supplemented the family's mainly grain, bean, and vegetable diet.

Because the Chinese considered milk the drink of barbarians, cattle, if a farmer owned any at all, were used solely to pull carts and plows. However, most farmers found that raising cattle was impractical in another way: Overgrazing by cattle promoted soil erosion, therefore jeopardizing the growth of crops on the farmer's land.

Farmers could hardly afford to lose any land to erosion. Throughout the Han empire, the average farm was relatively small, averaging only about seventy *mou,* or not quite a dozen acres. On this parcel of land, the farmer and his family were expected to grow enough to feed not only themselves but also to help keep the government's granaries well stocked. To this end, the emperor's bureaucrats over-saw the farmers' efforts. For example, in 168 B.C., in the face of a shortage of food reserves, an imperial edict admonished local officials to spur farmers to greater productivity. A model for fellow farmers to emulate was even provided with the selection of a *li-t'ien,* or "diligent cultivator," in each area. Han agricultural policy even extended to resettlement campaigns to increase the amount of land under cultivation.

In Debt

The life of a farmer was not only hard, it was also full of uncertainty. Either drought or flooding could destroy a harvest. Even when the weather cooperated and crops flourished, any political upheaval could disrupt farming duties. The *nong* could be drafted into the army to fight off invasion from outsiders like the nomadic Xiangnu tribes to the north or to quell some disturbance within the empire. Around the middle of the first century A.D., a children's song went,

> The wheat turns green;
> The barley withers.
> Who harvests the crop?
> Daughter-in-law and mother.
> Where is the man now?
> In the West, fighting the barbarians.[8]

A farmer's life could be disrupted by more than war or other unrest. Han emperors also saw the peasant population as a ready source of manpower. Thanks to an imperial system of labor conscription, men were obligated to serve in the government's labor corps, toiling on roads, canals, or other public-works projects.

Their livelihood under constant pressure from flood, drought, war, and public-works obligations, farmers battled debt continually.

Pottery warriors unearthed from a Han tomb. The Han army was staffed largely by the peasant population, or nong, *who were drafted during times of war or unrest.*

They frequently needed to borrow cash to buy seed for next year's crop. Making matters worse, the government, to avoid having to calculate crop yields each year, levied taxes not on what the land actually produced but according to the size of a farmer's plot of land. As a result, the farmer owed the same taxes, good year or bad. A difficult year or two could easily force him into bankruptcy.

When times were hard, his creditors could be counted on to show no mercy. To repay loans, a farmer might be forced to sell the very items he relied on to make his living—including his own children, who were a source of labor. Often, even this was not enough. After peddling his tools and livestock, and possibly selling his children into slavery, the farmer still might be unable to repay loans, since interest on such loans ran as high as 20 percent a year. His land then fell into the hands of his creditor. With few other options available to him, he would have little choice but to accept tenancy on a manor farm.

Tenancy

While tenancy offered some degree of security to a farmer, it came at a high price. The amount of land that he was allowed to work was barely a tenth of what he had previously owned. Furthermore, to work this piece of land—only on average about eight *mou* in size—the tenant farmer paid half of his produce in rent, the rest going to buying seed for the following year, paying taxes, and feeding his family. So poor was the tenant farmer, according to a commentator at the time, that he and his wife and children "ate the food of dogs and pigs."[9]

Owners of manor farms, by contrast, might be wealthy enough to live in two-storied homes with tiled roofs. The prosperity of the manor farm derived not only from its cheap labor—thanks to a steady supply of tenants— but also from its wide-ranging interests. Late in the Han dynasty, as the empire began to disintegrate, the manors developed more and more into self-sufficient units, from manufacturing their own lacquer furniture to mounting their own armed defense. During the war-torn years of the dynasty's decline, the manors were heavily fortified and manned. Guarded watchtowers loomed over estates throughout the land.

Even earlier in the Han dynasty, manor farms boasted resources that warranted protection supplied by walls. Tilled fields surrounded vegetable gardens that were in turn walled off to prevent livestock, whose stables and pens stood nearby, from eating the produce. Also nearby might be a mulberry grove where silkworms, which fed on the mulberry leaves, would be raised. Bamboo groves or date or citrus trees may have dotted the landscape as well. Along the banks of a fish pond, hemp was easily cultivated, providing the fibers needed for making rope. Clustered, too, around the manor's living quarters would have been granaries, sometimes raised on stilts to keep the grain inside dry and also safe from rats, as well as rooms for brewing wine and vinegar.

Grain grown on poorer farms was milled, or ground into flour, manually with a mortar and pestle or possibly with a circular millstone turned by a lever. On farming estates, this task was accomplished by yoking cattle or oxen to large grinding wheels. Tilt hammers were another device for crushing and pulverizing grain: A worker used his weight to shift the huge "hammer" backward and forward in a rocking motion.

Intensive Farming

To carry out the Han emperor's agricultural policy, which demanded maximum productivity, workers in the fields practiced intensive farming. Along with rigorous tilling, this process involved constant weeding, irrigating,

Farmers till the soil with an iron plow, a device owned by some Han farmers that eased the backbreaking work of tilling with hand tools.

and fertilizing. The output of labor required was enormous, but since a farmer's labor—whether independent or tenant—determined whether he and his family ate, a maximum effort was assured.

Hoes and even hands were employed for weeding, and hand tools were used by the *nong* for tilling. Spades had evolved from wooden digging sticks, sharpened at one end, with the addition of blades crafted from bone—usually the jawbone or shoulder blade of an ox—or, if provided by foundries owned by the imperial government, from iron. Whether single-tipped, double-pronged, or shovel-shaped, the spade made the task of breaking up the soil less wearisome, at least to a degree.

Farmers fortunate enough to have iron plows—also produced by imperial foundries—saved themselves much backbreaking work. The sharp triangular plowshares made the deep tilling of soil possible. Plows varied in size from so large that only a team of oxen could pull them to small enough to be wielded by a single person.

In much of China, rainfall fell short of agricultural needs, so farmers had to make the maximum use of what water they had available. An ancient proverb instructed farmers to always plow during a drizzle or after rain so as to conserve the moisture in the ground. Of course, irrigation allowed the farmer to regulate the supply of water, rain or shine. Most family farms during Han times had a well, which operated by means of a system of alternating buckets. Water poured from the buckets into a kind of tank built under the well frame. It then flowed out an opening in the tank into an irrigation trough or trench, which proceeded to deposit the water onto the fields. Even with the assistance of such mechanical devices, irrigating farmland was arduous work.

Like every other activity on the farm, irrigating the fields involved human labor, even when mechanical devices were in use. On large farming estates, water was often transported from low-lying irrigation ditches and canals into channels surrounding the fields by a kind of pump: Pedals turned a large cogwheel that pulled a chain of square wooden planks, and with them a stream of water, uphill. The work was arduous, but by use of their foot power, two people pedaling this device could irrigate hundreds of *mou*.

Chinese farmers were tremendously resourceful; fertilizers rich in phosphorous, potassium, and nitrogen were derived from composted plant matter and from animal, including human, waste. Weeds were cut, burned, and then drenched in water during the summer when the heat speeded up their decomposition. Additionally, toilets on farms were built so that pipes opened into an enclosure for easy collection of human waste. On some farms the toilets adjoined pigpens, so human and animal waste ended up conveniently in the same collection unit. The waste was then stored in stone jars or dried and reduced to a fine powder for treating the soil. Fertilizers usually underwent mixing with soil or other decaying plant matter before being applied to crops.

Time and Space

Intensive farming demanded efficiency as well as diligence on the part of the Han farmer. Sometime in the first century B.C., Zao Kuo, an agricultural official, developed an alternative to wastefully scattering seed in all directions when sowing. Known as *tai-tien*, this method channeled the seed into shallow furrows. Farmers were directed to plow their fields in a series of furrows, with the soil plowed up from each furrow forming an ac-

Workers use foot power to operate a sort of pump that helped ancient Chinese farmers accomplish the difficult task of irrigating farmland.

companying ridge. There in the furrow, the young plant was sheltered from the wind, while moisture was preserved in the soil as well as on the plant's leaves. Gradually, the ridges were pushed down to surround the root of the growing plant. As a bonus, farmers found well-aligned rows of plants easier to weed than the overcrowded clusters born of indiscriminate sowing.

Also for the sake of efficiency, farmers interplanted seeds. For example, they sowed millet with mulberry seed to supply the young mulberry trees with fertilizer—the ash of the burned millet stalk once the grain was harvested—while simultaneously making use of the space between the trees, which fortunately did not require much room to grow. In addition, Han farmers rotated crops, planting wheat, for instance, immediately after they harvested millet, and soybeans after they harvested wheat.

Timing was critical to the success of this intensive farming. Planting too early would yield a crop that grew stems and leaves instead of grain, and planting too late prevented the grain from maturing fully before the weather turned bad. The year was marked by the steps in the growing cycle: Cultivation took place in the spring, weeding in the summer, harvesting in the fall, and storage in the winter. Indeed, the labor, and lives, of farmers in ancient China followed closely the rhythm of the seasons. The stirrings of spring, around February, marked the beginning of the agricultural year.

By the (Text)Book

Farmers in Han times had written advice available to them. The following detailed directions for growing gourds, from a 20 B.C. textbook on agricultural methods, are excerpted in Michael Loewe's *Everyday Life in Early Imperial China*.

"Plough ten *mou* of good-quality land in the third month, and form into foot-square pits, each one foot deep. These should be pounded hard . . . so that they will retain water. The pits should be separated from each other by one pace [nearly nine inches]. Sow with four seeds each, and pack with one *tou* [about one quart] of silk-worm lime mixed with loam [moistened clay]. Sprinkle with two *sheng* [about half an ounce] of water. . . . When three fruit have set on each plant, beat with a horse-whip to prevent straggling growth. . . . Straw should be placed below the fruit to prevent them coming into contact with the soil and getting scabbed. . . . Gather the fruit in the eighth month [i.e., from mid-September] after the first light frosts."

Bamboo or mulberry trees might be transplanted or else carefully pruned. Manure was spread over fields, and melons, gourds, onions, and garlic could be sown.

The cycles of a farmer's life did not escape the attention of China's Han-era bureaucrats. Ts'ui Shih, a first-century A.D. official whose family had been landowners, published a guide to the different duties that a farm household ought to engage in throughout the year. In the second month, for example, a farmer was advised to practice his archery and so be prepared to fend off robbers. To further protect his household, he should repair his gates and doors.

Bureaucrats felt free to advise farmers on agricultural techniques as well. Ts'ui Shih recommended that the farmer break up heavy ground in the first month, more pliable earth in the second, and thin, sandy soils in the third. Throughout the first eight months some crop or other was to be sown, usually grains or beans, depending on the rainfall. Hay was to be harvested in the fifth month.

More of Ts'ui Shih's counsel is summarized by China scholar Michael Loewe:

Spring was a time for re-plastering the walls of the house and applying a fresh coat of lacquer where this was suitable. In the fifth month a farmer should remember that the seasonal rains would soon turn the lanes into an impassable quagmire, and it would be prudent to lay in a supply of food and firewood. . . . Granaries and storage pits should be repaired in the ninth month; and at the end of the year the far-sighted farmer would assemble his plough for the coming year's work and take care to feed his oxen to their fill, so that they would be fit and strong to face the labour of the working year that lay ahead.[10]

To Market

Ts'ui Shih's guidance extended to the production of clothing and textiles by the female members of the household. Summer tasks included washing old garments and cutting cloth for new ones. During the winter season, which could last as long as four months in the north, farmers' wives and daughters tirelessly spun and wove.

The women wove a variety of fabrics, but the most prized and most profitable was silk. Wherever mulberry trees could be grown, silkworms were raised—and carefully watched over—by the women of the farm. The silkworms' cocoons, once spun, were steamed, killing the worms and softening the silk fibers of their cocoons. To ensure a proper weave of silk cloth, the long threads from the cocoons had to be retrieved and spun onto spools in continuous lengths before they could spoil or be broken down by natural processes. Many households produced a variety of silks for sale, along with rougher fabrics, which were relegated to clothing worn by convicts. The extra cash earned from this textile trade helped farm families meet expenses.

A 17th-century illustration depicts Chinese women manufacturing silk. Silk-making techniques developed in ancient China continued in use almost to modern times.

Farmers sold other goods manufactured from field crops, too. Wine, for example, commanded a price twice that of the grain used to produce it. Preserved food, such as pickles and soybean paste, seasoned with spices gathered from the woods, could also be sold for profit. Herbs used for seasoning food, from leeks to ginger, provided still another source of income. Pigs raised on the farm could be brought to market as well.

The markets set up in China's ancient cities were bustling places where more than goods were traded. News and gossip were also exchanged. The local farmer, eager to supplement the family income by selling some specialty item or other, would have been fascinated with the variety of people he encountered there and with all they had to say about the larger world beyond his tiny hamlet.

2 In the City

Changan, the Han capital city, spread over the southern slope of a valley cut by the Wei River, a tributary of the mighty Huang He, through the heart of ancient China. The valley was crossed by busy trade routes. A farmer bringing goods to market in Changan would enter through one of its twelve gates, after first crossing a bridge over a moat twenty-four feet wide. As he crossed, above him loomed the city's walls, as much as sixty feet high in places. Up to fifty feet wide, the massive walls were built of rammed earth. The walls would have been awe-inspiring: Their total circumference was more than fifteen miles.

Taking into consideration both its natural and artificial barriers for defense, Han author Pan Ku boasted of the capital site, "It is the most impregnable refuge in heaven and earth."[11] Occupying each watchtower was a lookout whose job was to order the closing of the gate in anticipation of attack. On an ordinary day, guards allowed market-bound farmers to pass unchallenged through one of the gateway's three separate entrances. Each entrance was wide enough to admit four carriages side by side.

The roads leading into the city from the gates lay in parallel lanes corresponding to the three entranceways. The central lane, the

A tower along the city walls of modern-day Xi'an, site of ancient Changan. In contrast to the modern wall seen here, the city walls of Changan rose as high as sixty feet.

widest, was reserved for the emperor's use, forcing everyone else to use the two outer roads. Unpaved, these roads were dusty on dry days and muddy on rainy ones.

"As Closely as the Teeth of a Comb"

Once inside the city's walls, a visitor would find himself on one of Changan's eight major boulevards. The city was laid out in a rectangular grid of crisscrossing streets, compared by the poet Po Chü-i to a huge chessboard. The blocks formed by the intersecting streets were known as wards. Each ward was walled off from the others. Its gates were locked and guarded every evening, allowing authorities to keep a watchful eye on the imperial city's nearly quarter of a million inhabitants. The beating of drums warned inhabitants of the gates' closing each evening, and visitors from

Pastimes

Han city dwellers could choose from a variety of entertainments. Animals as well as humans performed for audiences. Dog and horse races were presented, along with brutal tiger and cock fights.

Those who had leisure time often spent it playing cards. Also popular were board games, including Chinese checkers and a game related to backgammon. Another board game, *liu-po,* also called "sixes," required two to four players. Taking turns, players shook six marked bamboo sticks like dice out of a cup and, depending on the throw, moved pieces around a board. Shouting and gesturing wildly apparently went along with playing *liu-po.* In works of Chinese art, the immortal beings, or gods, are sometimes shown absorbed in this game.

Children in Han China played jacks and a sport similar to badminton while adults often indulged in games of chance. However, high-stakes gambling, because it involved gaining wealth without producing anything of benefit to society, was frowned on by the imperial government, and those who engaged in it faced punishment.

A Han carving of two men playing the board game liu-po, *one of the many pastimes of the ancient Chinese.*

A Han dynasty model of a house, perhaps similar to the homes occupied by the artisans and tradespeople of the time.

distant wards, unable to complete the journey home through the city's maze of gateways, often had to make plans for an overnight stay away from home.

Most of Changan's 160 wards were residential, with most homes packed together "as closely as the teeth of a comb,"[12] according to a poet of the time. Reflecting the idea that the capital city's plan symbolized the universe and each person's place within it, where people lived in Changan indicated their status. Generally, the rich and powerful lived at one end of the city and the poorer, less-privileged population at the other.

Humble Homes

Visitors from the country would have found that the poorest of the city's inhabitants lived in homes that were little more than earthen pits: semiunderground, single-room dwellings barely seven feet by thirteen and a half feet. At the room's center stood a wooden pole supporting the circular thatched roof. The one room served both as living quarters and as kitchen.

Ancient Chinese tradition, based on the rudimentary compasses then in use, dictated that homes be built with a north-south orientation. The family generally slept in the northwest corner, on mats, their pillows consisting merely of planks of wood or chunks of pottery. At one wall was a fireplace, at the opposite wall a storage niche; on the central part of this wall a dirt ramp rose to ground level, leading to a wicker door. While damp on rainy days, this subterranean home at least offered warmth in the winter. The walls, hardened by fire, were plastered with yellow mud.

Similarly plastered were the walls of homes occupied by those on the next rung up the economic ladder, the artisans and tradespeople. Their simple houses were built at ground level on a minimally elevated foundation, which allowed for drainage. Each of the home's three separate rooms had its own individual entrance, the middle room higher and larger than those flanking it on either side. Unfinished timber, which was covered by

A modern illustration depicts a bustling Chinese marketplace from ancient times; at left is a member of the Chinese military; at right the watchtower guard keeps an eye out for invaders.

thatch reinforced by a layer of mud plaster, supported the roof.

A Profusion of Products

Changan's nine markets were located at the metropolis's north end, so farmers arriving from the countryside would likely have entered through one of the gates on that side of the city. A farmer arriving to sell his produce at one of the markets might hear, from its separate gateway, vendors advertising their wares or smell the food and drink offered at its myriad stalls, from tea to hot sausages. One Han writer reminisced about Changan's markets being so full of goods and people that there was no room for a person to turn his or her

head. Crowds of people mingled, including exotic-looking foreigners arriving on camels, all being entertained by jugglers, acrobats, puppeteers, and fortune-tellers. A profusion of products were available for sale: live animals, including pigs and sheep; fragrant foodstuffs, ranging from fresh fruits to pickled vegetables, relishes, and syrups. For the well-to-do shopper, pots and pans, gleaming metal tools, and lustrous fabrics such as silks and furs were all offered.

There was some order to the market's seeming chaos. Peddlers were ordered to leave the center clear, and set up their stalls around this space. Shops and stalls lay in rows, with traders bidding aggressively against one another. Those selling the same types of goods were assigned to the same quarter, which was supervised by a "head of the quarter," who collected the market tax and monitored the conduct of business. Over these heads of quarters, with the power of fixing price limits and granting or refusing the right to open a stall, was the "provost of the merchants." This official also had the honor of formally opening the market—by hoisting a flag above his office at the center of the square. This action was accompanied by a sounding of drums, which also marked the market's closing. Inspectors, meanwhile, kept an eye out for fraud. The market day itself was officially divided into three sessions: a morning session for wholesale dealers, an afternoon session relegated to farmers from

Wealthy Han women took great care with their appearance. They wore fine, embroidered clothing, elaborate hairstyles, and covered their faces with rice powder and makeup.

surrounding districts to sell their wares, and an evening session for small retailers.

All sorts of regulations attended the sale of goods. The length and width of rolls of silk, for example, were standardized. Also, the sale of fruits and grains was prohibited if they were out of season. Sales were confirmed by contract, although these were not always in written form. However, for more significant transactions, such as the buying of a slave, a formal deed of sale would be drawn up in duplicate by an official guaranteer, who levied a tax on the sale and judged any subsequent dispute.

Near evening farmers would leave the market, and their carts and wagons, which had been loaded with goods when they entered the city, would now be much lighter. Perhaps the departing farmers might catch a glimpse of shoppers arriving early for the evening session. Wealthy folk would pull up in carriages displaying gold or silver adornments. The horses pulling the carriages—each of which ate as much grain as a poor family of six—would be outfitted with jeweled breastplates and gilded or painted bridles.

Pointed or Curved?

No less adorned were the people stepping out of the carriages. Men's bronze belt hooks might be shaped like a tiger or a bird. Set in the bronze would be gold, silver, or semiprecious stones. Jade, gold, or silver hairpins glittered in women's hair.

Wealthy women fussed with makeup as well as their hairstyles. They covered their faces with rice powder and colored their cheeks, lips, and eyebrows. Their eyebrows were shaped by plucking unwanted hair with tweezers. The shape they chose for their eyebrows was dictated by fashion. A sharply pointed arch was the rage during early Han times in the second century B.C., while curved arches became fashionable a few hundred years later, near the end of the Han dynasty.

Both men and women of the wealthy class wore richly embroidered clothing. In winter, they wrapped themselves in furs. An official might wear a jacket of lamb's fur, with leopard skin cuffs. A jacket often topped the tunic that men wore over trousers. Women, as well as men on formal occasions, dressed in robes of fine silk.

"Long Happiness Without End"

The homes that these rich folk returned to after their trip to market were highly ornamented, with carved and painted facades, decorative tile, and pottery figures. A window opening might resemble the shape of some object or animal, and latticework window panels portrayed mythic figures and symbols in wood carvings. Latticework designs framing doors ranged from blossoms to geometric patterns. A pair of stone or granite lions often guarded the main doors of the homes of the rich, the male on the left sporting with a ball, the female on the right cradling a cub. Alternately, a set of stone drums, inset with mirrors, sat outside the main door. The door itself, constructed of hardwood, was often carved with deer, bats, and floral images symbolizing good fortune.

Also carrying a message of good fortune might be the home's roof tiles since the roof was believed to be a safeguard against evil spirits as well as weather. Tiles molded into half-cylinders from clay fired in kilns drained rainwater away in the troughs between them, and overhanging eaves guided the water clear of the home's outer walls. At the lower end of the roof, each half-cylinder was sealed with a roundel, or a circular tile end. This was generally decorated with some image—for example, a phoenix for good luck—or else Chinese characters spelling out some blessing such as "Long happiness without end."[13]

Tiles were often painted in colors ranging from yellow to gray. Color not only enlivened the appearance of a building but also symbolized certain abstract ideas. Ancient architectural records laid out the rules governing color symbolism. Green, for example, signified growth and long life whereas red represented good fortune and happiness. Colors were applied not only to tiles but also to structural wood elements, such as beams and columns. In addition to its symbolic value, paint on these elements served to protect the wood from decay.

"The Well of Heaven"

The abundance of timber in China made it a popular building material for city dwellers. It was also a practical one, given the danger of earthquakes. To help ensure that a building would withstand tremors—which were frequent—the most common construction method consisted of vertical posts supporting horizontal beams. A timber post-and-beam frame could flex whereas stone walls might collapse at the earth's violent shaking. Wooden posts, or columns, were arranged in specified patterns, each column given a particular name depending on its position. The shapes of columns varied from round to octagonal. The building's timber frame rested on a solid concrete or stone podium. This kept any dampness from rising up from the ground and rotting the wood. Generally, the higher the podium, the more important the person living in the house.

Another indication of status was whether the roof had two tiers or only one. A traditional feature of Chinese architecture was a

The wealthy class in Han China lived in elaborate homes which, like the more modern home illustrated here, featured latticework designs, two-tiered roofs, and courtyards.

roof that projected over the walls and tilted upward at the ends.

Also traditional to Chinese architecture was the courtyard. The courtyard of a home served various functions—from providing a source of light while preserving privacy to a way of ventilating as well as sectioning off the living space. Pots of flowers, shrubs, or a small tree might decorate a courtyard, along with a goldfish pond or simply a pool of water reflecting the clouds. This restful space was known as "the Well of Heaven." The home of a very rich or important person often had two courtyards, separated by a wall. A visitor might enter a home's surrounding wall through a gateway into an outer courtyard and be received there. However, someone close to the family could expect to be invited through another gate into an inner courtyard and the residence proper.

Multistoried Dwellings

Rooms along the sides of the outer courtyard generally housed guests or in-laws and sometimes the homeowner's personal library. The main building, reserved for the head of the household and his wife and children, stood at the far end of the inner courtyard. Separate from the main building, toward the back, huddled the servants' quarters.

Those wealthy enough to have servants often lived in multistoried homes, with balconies projecting from the upper floors. In summer, to let in more air, the waxed paper sheets covering windows were removed. At night, oil-fueled lamps provided light.

In the sleeping rooms, beds were spread with blankets stuffed with silk floss. Fine embroideries hung on the walls, and painted

Home visits were conducted with the utmost formality, no doubt owing to a book of etiquette edited during the Han dynasty that described the behavior expected of educated city dwellers. A formal exchange between guest and host is excerpted from this text in *Chinese Civilization and Society: A Sourcebook*, edited by Patricia Buckley Ebrey. Following protestations about who should be troubling to visit whom, the dialogue continues.

"The host: Since I have failed to receive permission to decline this honor [of receiving the guest], I shall not press it further. But I hear that you are offering me a gift, and this I must decline.

The guest: Without a gift I cannot dare to come into your presence.

The host: I am not worthy of these ceremonies, and so I must persist in declining.

The guest: If I cannot have the support of my gift, I dare not pay you this visit; so I persist in my request.

The host: I also am decided in declining, but as I cannot secure your consent, how dare I refuse?"

Bowing twice, the host meets the guest, who bows twice in response, at the gate. The host then invites the guest to enter into the courtyard, the host on the right, the guest on the left. There accepting the gift, the host bows twice, as does the guest. The guest then starts to leave, prompting the host to urge him to carry out his visit.

screens overlapped one another, offering privacy. Covering the floor here and throughout the house were wool or fur rugs and embroidered cushions. People also rested against these while dining since meals were taken while sitting on the floor. The kitchen was separated from the living quarters to keep the smell and noise of food preparation away. From its wood frame hung food and cooking utensils.

A "Harmony of Flavors"

Any number of dishes might be in preparation in the kitchen, including stewed turtle or a young roasted goat with yam sauce. When preparing meals, cooks employed by Changan's rich and powerful could choose from a bounty of ingredients. Their choice of vegetables, for example, ranged from farm- or garden-grown turnips, celery, cabbage, radishes, leeks, and onions to plants growing wild and gathered from meadows and forests, such as watercress and sowthistle, a kind of bitter herb. Available herbs and spices also included ginger—originally used to disguise the odor of spoiled meat—cinnamon, mustard, hot peppers, scallions, garlic, and shallots. Fish were generally seasoned with vinegar, pickles, salt, and plums in an attempt to achieve a major goal of traditional Chinese cooking: a "harmony of flavors."[14]

Along with a skillful mixing of flavors and ingredients, Chinese cooking featured minced, or bite-size, pieces. Occasionally, an entire animal—hair included—was roasted by Han cooks, but mostly meat was stripped off the bones and preserved by drying in the sun. It was then sliced or chopped before cooking, either as part of a stew or, for the richest families, as a main dish. In the following recipe, recorded from the Han period, the meat serves as a sauce base: "To prepare *hai* [boneless meat sauce] and *ni* [meat sauce with bones], it is necessary first to dry the meat and then cut it up, blend it with moldy millet, salt, and good wine, and place it in a jar. The sauce is ready in a hundred days."[15] Reflecting the sharp distinction between the city's rich and poor, while less well-off inhabitants of pit dwellings rarely tasted meat, Changan's wealthy classes feasted on wild boars, pigeons, elk, deer, ducks, and occasionally dogs, snakes, snails, and, as a delicacy, bear paws.

In contrast to the soups and stews eaten daily by most Han Chinese were "the Eight Delicacies," elaborate dishes reserved for the most privileged members of society. All involved painstaking preparation. For example, for what was called the Bake, a suckling pig or young ram was cut open, its entrails removed, and its belly stuffed with dates. Before being

A bear-footed bronze wine container from the Han dynasty. The use of bronze vessels in ancient China was restricted to food and beverages made from grains.

baked, the animal was wrapped in straw and reeds, which were in turn covered over with clay. Once baking was complete, the clay was broken off. Crackling, or crisped fat from the skin, was mixed with rice flour and smeared over the animal, which was then deep fried. Finally, the meat was sliced and then boiled for a period of three days and nights in water filled with herbs.

People living during the Han period regarded the element of metal as antagonistic to the element of fire, so even the very rich, who could well afford an entire kitchen of bronze utensils, scrupulously avoided them for certain uses. The ever-present bureaucracy dictated what type of food could come in contact with what type of material. To conform to these regulations, bronze vessels were apparently restricted to food and drink made from grains.

The ancient Chinese drew symbolic correlations between the elements water, fire, wood, metal, and earth; the five directions of north, south, east, west, and central; the four seasons; and categories of tastes, smells, domestic animals, and grains. Based on such correlations, meals became a ritual experience. Within the emperor's palace, meals were served with such exacting ritual that the position of a fish on a serving plate depended on the season of the year.

Inspiring Awe

Changan, as the capital city, bore the unmistakable stamp of the imperial presence. Given its association with the emperor, who mediated between earthly and heavenly realms, the city was planned keeping in mind correspondences between the ordering of the earth and the wider universe. The expectation was that a capital city designed in keeping with cosmic principles would compel obedience

Table Manners

Rules for dining reflected the highly stratified society found in a major Han city like Changan. For example, while a high-ranking minister might be entitled to eight dishes of grain, a lower-ranked official could expect only six. A guest dining with someone of superior rank was advised to take small and frequent mouthfuls, chewing quickly; he also was admonished not to make faces or noises, such as crunching bones with his teeth, while chewing.

Other prohibitions for guests wanting to make a good impression included not putting back on the serving platter fish they had been eating, not rolling the grain they were served into a ball, not swilling the soup, not throwing bones to the dogs, and not picking their teeth. When finished eating, they were instructed to kneel and begin removing dishes, handing them to attendants, until the host rose and declined this service; only then could they resume their seats.

from the emperor's subjects. Consequently, Changan seems to have been laid out to reflect the position of the stars in the constellation that is known to many today as the Big Dipper. Moreover, the emperor's palace was built so that when sitting in his audience hall, he faced south, the domain of the positive force of yang.

The Han imperial complex, besides dozens of palaces and shrines, included several gardens and parks. In them, weeping willow tree branches trailed picturesquely in man-made lakes. Here and there, pavilions invited restful contemplation. Some parks were simultaneously hunting grounds and zoological gardens. In these parks the emperor could hunt animals from all over his realm, signifying his power over all creatures. Hunting was the primary pastime of the emperor and his court. Their prey included tigers, panthers, bears, wolves, buffalo, and wild boars. Bushes that the animals might use for cover would be set on fire, and the hunters then pursued their quarry either on foot or by chariot. Members

of the imperial hunting party outfitted themselves in hats decorated with pheasant tails and pants made of white tiger skin.

The imperial compound dominated the capital city. In fact, most of the gates leading into the south of Changan were used exclusively to leave or enter the compound. The compound itself accounted for much of the city's southern and central sections. Within the compound, palaces were sometimes enormous. The Weiyanggong, for example, a palace built prior to the rest of the city while the Han dynasty was still consolidating its rule, was one-seventh the size of the whole of Changan.

The dynasty's founder, Gaozu, himself questioned this excess, demanding to know, "Why are palaces constructed so much beyond their proper limits?"[16] Evidently, the palace architects aimed to build structures inspiring awe. Awe was understood to be a proper reaction to an emperor of ancient China, believed as he was to possess ultimate, even divine, authority.

CHAPTER 3

In Power

The title the Han emperors adopted from their Qin predecessors, *huangdi*, expressed their near-divine power; the term *huang*, meaning "radiant, illustrious, glorious," was associated with the legendary god-kings of still earlier times. The emperor's personal name, intimately associated with his sacred person, could never, out of deference, be spoken, not even by his ministers. Instead, he was addressed by his title or indirectly, by referring to his chariot—that is, *ch'eng-yü*.

In keeping with the emperor's exalted position, his way of life was unique in all of China. First of all, he inhabited the innermost part of a closely guarded complex of palaces, attended to by a host of servants and courtiers. Failing to

Ancient Chinese emperors occupied an exalted position. Any person who failed to show proper respect in their presence faced harsh and certain punishment.

show the emperor proper respect in his presence meant certain punishment. For example, a nobleman accused of dressing casually when invited to the palace abruptly lost his rank. Visitors arriving uninvited faced execution, and that included nobles and officials as well as common folk.

Further setting the emperor apart, ritual governed his daily habits. As heaven's representative on Earth, he had to ensure that his every action harmonized with the great cosmic cycles reflected in nature. As viewed by the ancient Chinese, these cycles corresponded to the seasons of the year, as correlated with colors and with the directions north, south, and so on. Therefore, in spring the emperor took up residence in the Eastern Pavilion and wore green; in summer he moved to the Southern Pavilion and clothed himself in red. In autumn his home was the Western Pavilion and his wardrobe was white; in winter he relocated to the Northern Pavilion and dressed all in black.

Emperor Gaozu, founder of the Han dynasty. Gaozu, whose name means "Great Ancestor," came from peasant stock.

Diet also played into this system, so that the season of the year determined the ingredients of the emperor's meals. Dog meat and hemp seed, for example, because of their metaphysical significance in Han times, were on the imperial menu for autumn.

The Son of Heaven

The emperor's unique lifestyle derived from both the privileges and responsibilities that he assumed as the *t'ien tzu*, or "son of heaven." This title confirmed that he was subject only to heavenly powers, every other living creature being subservient to him. However, it also implied that his position was secure only as long as those powers remained favorable to him and his rule.

The *t'ien-ming*, or "mandate of heaven," formalized this doctrine, holding that just as any worthy candidate could be granted the authority to govern, if he showed himself unfit for this responsibility, it would promptly be taken from him. In other words, the emperor's continued enjoyment of power and prestige depended on the success of his guardianship of the people and the land.

The founder of the Han dynasty, Gaozu, acknowledged his debt to the mandate in the following anecdote:

> So often did [the minister] Lu Chia quote from the *Book of Odes* and the *Book of History* [classical texts believed to be edited by the moral teacher Confucius] that Emperor [Gaozu] became annoyed and said, "I conquered the Empire on horseback. What is the good of these *Odes* and *Histories?*" Lu Chia replied, "That is correct but you won't be able to govern on horseback. . . . If [Qin], having made itself the master of the Empire, had governed it

in humanity and righteousness, if it had followed the precepts of the ancient sages, then Han would not have got it." The Emperor blanched and said, "Explain to me the reasons for the collapse of [Qin] and the rise of Han as well as what it was that won and lost kingdoms of old."[17]

Peacocks and Poisons

This anecdote emphasizes one consequence of the mandate: government based on accountability. At the same time, the mandate's conditional nature exposed the dynasty to superstition and intrigue. Recognizing that their position came without a guarantee, Han emperors anxiously consulted with those who studied the earth and sky for signs of heaven's judgment on their rule. In the process, some of these court functionaries made scientific observations, keeping systematic records of sun spots and tracking the appearance of comets. Others kept watch for more mystic signs, from the unearthing of a rusting sword to the hatching of a white peacock. Interpreting such omens for the emperor, diviners guided him in taking action believed necessary to maintain his rule.

Suspect as the advice of diviners may have been, ultimately more destructive to the dynasty was the poisoning of the atmosphere at court by the spread of factions, all plotting for power. The eldest son of the empress could generally expect to be appointed heir apparent—that is, the person who would ascend to the throne when the current emperor died. However, the empress's position (and that of her offspring) was far from secure. She could suddenly be dismissed by order of the emperor or even handed poison and commanded to commit suicide. Succession, and therefore the continuity of the dynasty, often depended

Monitoring the Mandate

In the belief that natural phenomena, including comets, eclipses, and earthquakes, signaled heaven's displeasure, Han scientists were often employed at court to monitor such happenings. An ingenious mathematician and astronomer who was also a civil servant, Zhang Heng (A.D. 78–139), improved current techniques for tracking ominous events above or below ground. For example, he constructed an armillary sphere, or model of the sky, allowing it to be measured and mapped.

Probably one of Zhang Heng's most intriguing devices was a seismograph, or tool for detecting earthquakes. Invented in about A.D. 130, it could locate tremors at a distance of several hundred miles as well as indicate their direction. Inside the circular bronze machine, measuring a good six feet across, a pendulum vibrated during an earthquake. This vibration triggered the release of a ball from the mouth of one of eight dragon heads; the ball dropped out of the machine into the mouth of a frog squatting below. The clang of the ball dropping sounded an alarm, and the particular dragon that had released the ball pointed to the direction of the quake.

on the ever-shifting relationships of the emperor and his many wives and concubines.

Among these women, the competition to be appointed empress, or imperial consort, could be fierce and even deadly. The Han historian Pan Ku relates the following conversation between a woman doctor, addressed as Shao-fu, who attended the pregnant Empress Hsü, and Ho Hsien, the wife of a military official at court:

Mother Knows Best

A woman in ancient China rarely had political power of her own and remained subservient to the male members of her family. The one exception was the empress, whose status gave her power over her male relatives. Ironically, this power increased when her husband, the emperor, died, and her title was elevated to that of empress dowager. The empress dowager Tou, for example, when angry at her older brother, ordered him confined to the palace.

An empress dowager played an active role in the government if the new emperor, her son, was still a boy. Sometimes her power lasted even into his young adulthood. In theory, she ruled jointly with the emperor; but in fact, she wielded considerable political control, issuing edicts in her own name and appointing officials. For instance, the empress dowager Lü began the practice of attending court and so dominated the government that her son, Emperor Hui, was completely ignored in official histories of the dynasty. In another case, Emperor Wudi's mother, in the early years of his reign, executed tutors whose teaching she opposed, and because of the Chinese custom of a son obeying his mother, he made no protest. Wudi saw, however, the danger posed by the empress dowager's power. Nearing death, Wudi decreed that his widow be executed to avoid her interfering with the rule of her son, the new emperor. Several later emperors followed Wudi's example.

Hsien said, "My husband the general in chief has always been extremely fond of our youngest daughter, Ch'eng Chün, and would like to see her given some position of special honor. We would like you to help us, Shao-fu."

"What do you mean?" asked [Shao-fu].

"It is a very serious thing for a woman to give birth," said Ho Hsien. "Hardly one woman out of ten survives. Now the empress is about to bear a child. It would be quite possible to put poison in her medicine and do away with her, and then Ch'eng Chün could be made empress in her place. If you agree to help and the affair is successful, you may be sure that we will share the wealth and honor with you, Shao-fu!"[18]

The selection of a relative to be imperial consort was probably the quickest route to political advancement and its associated privileges in Han times. A father or brother of a new empress frequently enjoyed appointment to a prize post—no matter how humble his background. For example, Wei Ch'ing, a servant when his sister became the emperor's consort, was immediately appointed a general and eventually elevated to the ranks of nobility.

Ranking

Plagued as it was by plotting and intrigue, the imperial court was still the center of power in Han China. Officials of the central government consulted with the emperor in determining major policy, including how order was to be kept inside the country as well as along its borders. One top official, the imperial chancellor—corresponding roughly to the prime minister of a modern-day nation—enjoyed unparalleled access to the emperor in forming such policies. In fact, the emperor was known to pay a visit to the imperial chancellor when this minister was ill. No other person at court could expect such an honor.

The rank below that of imperial chancellor included several ministry or department heads. These high-ranking officials oversaw the operation of government as well as the imperial household. Every department head supervised a number of underlings assigned to often seemingly unrelated bureaus or sections carrying out specific tasks. The "keeper of the imperial purse," for example, headed a section responsible for the craftsmen who designed the palace furnishings. Another section was charged with preparing the badges

Sculptures of military officials from the more recent Tang dynasty. In Han China, such an official's rank determined his status in society.

worn by officials to mark their rank: a series of gold, silver, and bronze seals, decked with purple, blue, yellow, or black ribbons according to the official's position and salary—because rank was key to so many aspects of life at court, having a way to identify a person's standing was critical.

The officials of the central government, located at the capital city, formed one arm of imperial rule; the other consisted of provincial functionaries scattered throughout China. The provincial government was itself organized into two branches: commanderies and principalities. These were political entities as well as territorial divisions of the empire. Commanderies were a construct of the imperial bureaucracy, designed purely to serve administrative ends. They were overseen by grand administrators, who were appointed by the central government. Principalities were maintained to honor kinship ties—as the word suggests, they were ruled by princes, all of whom were related by blood to the emperor. Positions in the provincial administration remained unstable throughout the Han era, as principalities were invariably eliminated, reduced in size, or split up depending on who sat on the imperial throne and to however many relatives he owed favors. In theory, the rule of a principality was hereditary; in reality, though, the central government manipulated this process to serve its own ends, along with appointing the prince's senior assistant. In the end, then, the central government had as much direct control over the principalities as over the commanderies.

Both commanderies and principalities were divided into smaller units, called prefectures. Prefectures were themselves broken up into districts, and districts were divided into wards. Some government duties could be delegated to the minor, or local, officials of districts, wards, or prefectures, who all shared the task of putting into action the policies of the central government. Local officials, for example, made sure that grain was stored against times of famine and that granaries, along with roads and canals, were in good repair. In addition, these officials served as both civilian and military police, arresting criminals and army deserters, as well as anyone who dared shelter such lawbreakers. In fact, the bulk of the work of government was carried out by these minor officials. In cooperation with provincial authorities, they were also expected to manage the system of communications vital to the operation of a government spread out over such a large area as China. Urgent messages as well as routine mail traveled from one locally maintained station to another by messengers mounted on horseback or traveling on foot.

Competition

Even these minor government positions provided opportunities for advancement for those with ambition and talent. Reportedly, a humble runner named K'ung Sung, "who was upright and strict in morals,"[19] received a summons to the capital and eventually achieved the post of grand administrator. Beginning in 196 B.C., it had become an annual event for each commandery and principality to send a certain number of promising young men to the capital city, where they could be considered for government posts. By the middle of the first century A.D., a quota had been fixed; for example, for every two hundred thousand inhabitants, a commandery submitted one candidate chosen for his upright behavior and devotion to family and between six and ten candidates familiar with the Confucian classics dealing with morality and statecraft.

In fact, the Han dynasty promoted the development of the world's first civil service. In

A.D. 124, Emperor Wudi founded an imperial university in the capital city as a training institute for aspiring civil servants, and the Confucian classics constituted the curriculum. These included the *Book of Changes,* a "how-to" book on divination; the *Book of History,* an account of the speeches and deeds of the leg-

Up and Down the Bureaucratic Ladder

An official's ranking in the government bureaucracy invariably determined his prestige in society. Therefore, a promotion or demotion meant a change in status. Such a reversal, reflected in the shifting attitude of others toward him, is illustrated in the experience of bureaucrat Su Ch'in, presented by T'ung-tsu Ch'u in his book *Han Social Structure.*

"When Su Ch'in did not succeed in getting an appointment, his brothers and their wives, and his sisters, wife, and concubines all ridiculed him. Later when he became chancellor of the Six Kingdoms and returned home, his brothers and their wives and his own wife waited upon him at dinner, prostrating themselves and not daring to raise their faces to look at him. He asked his brother's wife, 'Why were you so haughty before and so humble now?' She crawled on hands and knees with her face touching the ground and apologetically said, 'Because you have a high post and plenty of gold.' Then Su Ch'in sighed and said, 'Although the same person, when one is rich and honorable he is feared by his relatives, but when he is poor and humble he is treated lightly. How much more so with other people.'"

Emperor Wudi (in foreground at left) founded an imperial university in Changan, the ancient capital, in order to train outstanding young men who aspired to government posts.

endary kings of the distant past; the *Book of Odes* (or *Book of Poetry*), a collection of folk poetry interpreted as having hidden moral meaning; the *Spring and Autumn Annals,* a history of Confucius's own home state, Lu; and the *Book of Ritual,* a manual of proper behavior for everyone from peasant to ruler.

Candidates for civil service were required to pass a series of rigorous exams involving questions about the Confucian classics, whose over 425,000 words they had to memorize. Each candidate spent days closely guarded in one of a vast number of tiny rooms set aside to house the many hopefuls gathered in the capital. Those candidates who managed to receive a passing grade joined a pool of office seekers waiting at court for an assignment; sometimes these numbered as many as a thousand at a time.

When there was finally an opening and someone was appointed to the post, he first served for a trial period. After a year he could consider the assignment permanent. Most

likely he would be given the routine tasks of a clerk or provincial civil servant. Staffing the various government agencies, these low-ranking functionaries were buried in paperwork. In the confines of their offices, they busied themselves either receiving or drafting reports or keeping tax records. Meanwhile, they were subjected to continued scrutiny by their supervisors.

A report submitted by provincial authorities every three years included a grading of their subordinates. Specified was the name and position of the functionary; an evaluation of his service as "high," "medium," or "low"; an indication of how long he had spent in this particular post; certification of his ability to read, write, and manage accounts and his familiarity with the laws; his height and age; and the distance his place of service was from his hometown. This last entry showed obedience to the rule forbidding service in someone's home district, a safeguard against the temptation to perform favors for friends and relatives.

All government officials had to pass a series of rigorous exams. This 18th-century painting shows candidates taking the examination to become country magistrates, just as their ancient counterparts did 1500 years earlier.

Promotion or demotion often followed the submission of these reports, usually to the position immediately above or below whatever post was currently held. Sometimes an official rose automatically to the next level after a certain length of duty. Occasionally, thanks to an imperial edict, an exceptional individual might jump ahead several ranks. On the other hand, an official shown to be neglectful of his duties or incompetent or charged with a crime faced demotion or even dismissal.

A promotion might mean transfer to the hub of central government from the backwater of provincial service. It might even mean an audience with the emperor. Imperial audiences were governed by strict rules of conduct. The official arrived at the designated gate of the palace at the appointed time, dressed in his proper robe and cap, with his badge of office clearly displayed. Departing his carriage, he would make his way to the imperial presence on foot and also on the double, to demonstrate his zest for his work and his determination to serve.

A "Previous Request"

Promotions also meant an increase in pay; in fact, civil service positions were graded according to salary. These gradings were stated in terms of a yearly allowance of measures of grain—though salaries were also paid partly in coin and sometimes in the form of bolts of silk. If an official retired honorably because of old age, he might receive bonuses at the time in money or silks. On occasion, he was granted a retirement income, possibly one-third of his annual salary at his final post.

A top-ranking official could gain considerable wealth. One grand administrator of a commandery, for example, owned eight hundred household slaves. Lavish displays of the material benefits of office, from spacious homes to expensive fox furs, served a calculated purpose: to encourage China's best and brightest to compete for posts. In fact, early on in the Han period, most newly appointed officials were rough-and-ready military men who cared little for finery. A regulation therefore subjected to punishment those whose clothing, carriage, and supply of horses failed to suit their status in the government hierarchy.

Beyond the opportunity to live in style, officials enjoyed a number of other privileges. For example, if they were accused of a crime, their arrest had to be approved by the emperor, a practice known as *hsien-ch'ing*, or "previous request." Furthermore, those who could afford to, when convicted of a crime, could often ransom themselves from physical punishment by paying fines or choosing exile.

Crime and Punishment

Being accused of committing a crime was a fearsome thing in ancient China, particularly since the accused was presumed guilty until proven innocent. The accused was immediately arrested and thrown into prison, sometimes in chains. An official interrogation followed in which the prisoner might be tortured to obtain a confession. Witnesses were called, and to ensure that they showed up at the trial, they faced being locked up in a prison cell.

Influence and Advancement in the Emperor's Service

Although individuals were supposed to be recommended for government posts based on merit, critics of the system claimed that friends, relatives, and those of wealth and influence were often promoted over better-qualified candidates. This excerpt from an essay by Wang Fu (ca. A.D. 100–150), in editor Patricia Buckley Ebrey's *Chinese Civilization and Society: A Sourcebook*, attacks the assumption that only the worthy were promoted.

"The poor scholar, being in a humble position, has much to bear. . . . At banquets his gifts are small and considered inadequate. His own parties are simple and not up to others' standards.

Those who burn for rapid promotion and advancement . . . scrape and claw to make their way to the front but have little time to concern themselves with those who have been left behind. . . . This is the reason that crafty, calculating individuals can worm their way up the official ladder while ordinary scholars slip ever more into obscurity.

Alas! The gentlemen of today speak nobly but act basely. . . . When they actually recommend people for office, they consider only such requirements as influence and prominence. If a man is just an obscure scholar, . . . even if he is modest and diligent, . . . even if he is filled with the most devoted compassion for the people, he is clearly not going to be employed in this world."

Once all relevant testimony and evidence were considered, the charge was read to the accused, who could request further inquiry. Once a guilty judgment was reached, the convicted criminal was sentenced to punishment. An effort was made to assign a punishment appropriate for the crime. For example, if a murder or assault were committed with a tool ready-at-hand, such as an awl or hoe—that is, if the crime were not premeditated—the punishment was less severe than if a sword or dagger, which had to be drawn from its sheath, was used.

The death penalty was carried out by beheading the victim or chopping him or her in two at the waist. Physical punishment often involved mutilation, including tattooing the forehead or cheeks or, for more serious crimes, cutting off some body part or other. Such mutilations were a terrible disgrace because the human body was considered a gift from one's parents. Marring and disfigurement, therefore, displayed for all to see the seriousness of one's offense.

Statutes, Ordinances, and Registers

Justice in ancient China also might be meted out in accordance with still more ancient traditions. In the more remote districts of the empire, respect for the deep-rooted authority of village elders probably held more sway than did the laws of the emperor. In a number of cases, the persuasive powers of these honored individuals resolved conflicts before the complexities of the Han legal code could even be applied.

Nevertheless, even in remote areas officials were forced to take action following certain crimes. These included dishonoring the emperor, such as ridiculing him in some way; interfering with the functioning of government, such as forging official documents or accepting bribes; or committing violent acts, such as murder or assault. Such infractions violated imperial statutes or ordinances and thus could not be ignored.

Statutes and ordinances—bearing such titles as the Statute on Banditry, the Statute on Gold and Coins, and the Ordinance Concerning Ritual Fasts—conveyed the emperor's general policies for governing the public. Some ordinances, issued in series such as Ordinance A, Ordinance B, and so on, addressed such policies as irrigation and care of the elderly. Copies of statutes and ordinances were periodically compiled and distributed to provincial authorities, bringing them up-to-date with the emperor's will.

The government, meanwhile, passed its decisions on specific matters through the bureaucratic chain of command in the form of edicts bearing the emperor's signature. Edicts addressed a wide variety of matters, from arrangements for tax collection and repair of dams to the bestowal of bounties, which were rewards or subsidies offered now and then by the emperor to individuals as well as to families and other groups of people and even to the mass of his subjects. For example, bounties might extend amnesty to criminals or aid to an area devastated by an earthquake or flood. Sometimes bounties were granted on state occasions, such as the naming of an heir apparent to the imperial throne, to drum up public enthusiasm for such events.

Also helping administrators to manage China's population were the registers of land and households. Conducted yearly, these censuses made it possible for the government to draw on the population as a source of revenue and manpower. Land registers identified property held in a person's name and provided a general grading of its quality—as good, medium, or poor—information needed to levy an appropriate tax. The standard rate

Peasants express their humility by bowing to a magistrate. Even in remote areas, all individuals were expected to adhere to the imperial statutes and ordinances, or face harsh and swift punishment.

of the land tax was usually one-thirtieth of the produce estimated for that grade of land, regardless of other factors that affected productivity. Household registers, meanwhile, were used to assess the government's other primary source of revenue: the poll tax, generally levied at a rate of 120 five-*shu* coins per adult and twenty-three such coins for each child between the age of seven and fourteen. These registers listed the name, sex, and relationship of each member of a household.

Besides facilitating the collection of taxes, the registers gave the government an idea of the manpower currently available to call into service. Beginning at age twenty-three and continuing to age fifty-six, males were liable for service one month annually in the government labor corps—though they were probably not called up every year, and officials above a certain rank were exempt. This labor pool was required for public works, such as building or repairing roads or constructing massive tombs for the emperor and his family. Males identified as eligible by the registers were also obligated to serve in the emperor's army.

4 At War

As long as he was physically able, from the age of twenty-five to sixty, the average man in ancient China was required to be available to serve in the nation's army. He generally served a term of two years. If he saw battle, he did so as an infantryman, or foot solider, bearing the brunt of the fighting. The cavalry, who fought on horseback, were most likely volunteers: those privileged members of society, such as nobles and officials, who enjoyed exemption from conscription. The size of the army in the late Han period is estimated at 130,000 to 300,000 men.

The grand administrator of a commandery received orders in writing to call out troops for a specific purpose. Troops might be sent to put down a rebellion somewhere in the empire or possibly conduct a campaign of

A Tang dynasty cave painting depicts a Chinese cavalry. Han dynasty cavalry were usually made up of high-ranking nobles and officials.

conquest. Han emperors boldly sponsored military ventures into Korea, for instance, intent on colonization. (Difficulties in maintaining communications and supplies eventually brought such expeditions to a standstill.)

The Han army was able to launch such large-scale operations because of its high degree of organization. Lists of officers and their troops, with details including name, age, status, and birthplace, were scrupulously drawn up. In addition, achievement records were kept on officers, from how they went about their duties to their performance on annual archery tests. Moreover, financial accounts and inventories of weapons and supplies were carefully maintained. Inspectors' reports noted the condition of watchtowers and the competence of the guards who manned them.

General Directions

The army's tight organization nevertheless allowed generals considerable leeway in how they managed their troops. Li Kuang and Ch'eng Pu-chih both held commands in about 140 B.C., though their styles, as described in Burton Watson's translation of selections from Pan Ku's history of the period, differed widely:

> When Li Kuang went out on expeditions . . . he never bothered to form his men into battalions and companies. He would make camp wherever he found water and grass, leaving his men to set up their quarters in any way they thought convenient. He never had sentries circling the camp at night and . . . he kept records and other clerical work down to a minimum.
>
> Ch'eng Pu-chih, on the other hand, always kept his men in strict battalion and company formation . . . his officers

worked over their records and reports until dawn, and no one in his army got any rest. Ch'eng Pu-chih once expressed the opinion, "Although Li Kuang runs his army in a very simple fashion, if the enemy should ever swoop down on him suddenly he would have no way to hold them off. His men enjoy plenty of idleness and pleasure, and for that reason they are eager to fight to the death for him. Life in my army may be a good deal more irksome, but at least I know that the enemy will never catch me napping!"[20]

When in battle, the leader of a company signaled an advance with a drum beat and a retreat with a chiming of bells or gongs. His banner, mounted high on his chariot, served as a rallying point for his troops, as he oversaw operations from the vantage point of the chariot's boxlike platform while a charioteer maneuvered the vehicle. Between these two, a warrior stood ready with a weapon—either a spear, bow and arrow, or axlike halberd—to protect them as well as the horses.

Beasts of Battle

The Chinese war chariot was drawn by up to four horses fitted with an efficient collar harness system. The harness, along with the vehicle itself, was decorated to heighten the spectacle of the horse and chariot in battle. While they still served as symbols of strength and military might, chariots eventually proved too cumbersome to play a major tactical role in campaigns, particularly in rough terrain.

Horses, however, continued to be valued on the battlefield as mounts for the cavalry. More mobile than war chariots and better able to handle uneven ground, the cavalry increasingly took an active role in offensive as

Although an imposing sight, Chinese war chariots were too cumbersome to play an important offensive role in battle.

well as defensive maneuvers. While chariots stuck close to the infantry, which functioned as the company's main body, the cavalry rode loosely alongside the infantry's flanks. From this position, they could defend more vulnerable foot soldiers or be dispatched for lightning-quick attacks against the enemy.

Poised for action in the saddle—which was made of leather and metal and was decorated with ribbons—the cavalrymen cut dashing figures. Enhancing the impression that they made were the prized horses the emperor Wudi secured for them; previously they had ridden smaller Mongolian ponies. By raiding the famed horse breeders of Ferghana (now the central Asian nation of Uzbekistan) as well as by swapping one of his female relatives for a thousand horses from a barbarian king, Wudi was able to breed the magnificent animals. Still, even after over three hundred thousand were bred, a decent mount was so valuable that it could command three hundred pounds of gold.

Putting on Protection

A full-size horse could carry a more heavily armored calvaryman than a pony could. At the same time, advances in iron making during

The Art of War

"War is that matter which is most vital to the state. It is the province of life or death, and the path which leads to survival or to ruin." Quoted in *The First Emperor of China*, by R. W. L. Guisso et al., these are the opening words of *The Art of War*, the classic Chinese guide to strategy and tactics that dates from about the fifth century B.C. First annotated during Han times, the work is attributed to Sun Zi, a military strategist and general during the Warring States Period. Supposedly studied by Napoléon and cited by Mao Zedong, its relevance persists. Strategies derived from *The Art of War* have been adapted to modern computer games, and commuters riding Japan's subways can be seen reading from its pages in comic book form.

According to *The Art of War*, warfare is not confined to the battlefield. Instead, war is ultimately a kind of mind game, with its objective being psychological dominance over an opponent. It counsels knowing one's enemy in order to exploit his strengths and weaknesses to one's advantage. The goal is to disorient the enemy so that he is no longer able to make intelligent decisions or to think clearly, thus making him vulnerable to defeat.

A detail from a 12th-century scroll painting depicting early Han dynasty soldiers subduing the enemy. The ancient Chinese recognized the importance of strategy both on and off the battlefield.

the Han period were improving the strength and quality of armor. The skill of Han iron-workers produced a kind of fish-scale suiting—in some cases consisting of over twenty-five hundred separate plates—that flexed and moved with the body. However, such intricately wrought pieces were reserved for the higher-ranking mounted soldier; the mass of peasant troops were outfitted with leather plates lacquered and laced together with leather thongs.

The style as well as material making up the armor differed depending on the soldier's ranking. On officers, rectangular iron scales or plates were layered over a leather foundation and a wide-sleeved robe and a bright cape with tassels hung from the shoulders. Only the upper body was armored, generally with a breastplate and often with a section protecting the back. Occasionally, pieces shielding the shoulders and upper arms were attached to this main section of armor. Charioteers' armor included jointed sleeves to protect the arms without hampering their ability to control the vehicle. The cavalry, meanwhile, wore short vestlike armor, practical for riding. The infantry was outfitted with a leather panel that covered the chest and groin and was held in place by crossed straps at the back. A linen scarf prevented the armor from chafing the wearer's neck.

The protection afforded a soldier above the neck also varied by rank. Officers and charioteers wore bonnetlike headgear while the cavalry sported soft caps secured with chin straps. Foot soldiers generally went bareheaded.

Deadly Developments

Armor was highly developed by the time of the Han dynasty. Advancements in weapons beginning in the bloody civil wars of the Warring States Period had made improvements in armor necessary. Probably the most significant of these "improved" instruments of war was the crossbow. Foot soldiers armed with this deadly device could repel an infantry

Kites as Weapons

Kites evidently originated with the Han Chinese military. The first reference to a kite is in an account about a Han general, Hsin, who died in 196 B.C. The wily general ordered a kite flown over enemy lines so that, from the length of its string, he might judge the distance between his army and the enemy. With that measurement, he was able to determine how long a tunnel his troops would need to dig to reach that site. Kites were also used as strategic devices by Chinese armies, particularly to signal messages. Since they were put to practical uses, these early kites appear to have been limited to simple rectangular shapes.

Apparently, military strategy also led to the development of the first wind psaltery, or windpipe kite—that is, a kite equipped with whistles or panpipes. Early on in the Han period, a general still loyal to the previous regime, the Qin, found his army hemmed in by Han troops. As a means of escape, he came up with the idea of causing panic among his adversaries by flying kites, to which bamboo pipes were attached, over their camp late at night. The whistling sound resulting from the wind passing through the pipes reportedly resembled *"Fu Han!"* meaning "Beware, Han!" The Han troops, interpreting this sound as guardian spirits warning them of impending doom, promptly fled.

An illustration of a Han battle shows soldiers using many of the tools and weapons of war available at the time, including chariots, armor, crossbows, and swords.

charge with a hail of short, heavy arrows—firing as far as 650 feet to penetrate an infantryman's wooden shield. Unlike the longbow, whose power was limited by how far the archer could draw the string, the crossbow's string was pulled back with both hands and locked in place. A trigger then released the string, firing a lethal shot with less effort and greater speed than would have been possible using muscle power alone.

For the crossbow to be accurate, the triggers and other component parts had to be carefully made. During the Han period, bronze trigger mechanisms were standardized in government foundries. According to scholar Michael Loewe,

These instruments were made with a very considerable degree of precision, and comprised several component parts that were fitted together with the greatest accuracy. A catch, which held the bowstring, and a control lever which released the arrow were fitted by means of pins to a principal box-like part; and some triggers were equipped with a graduated sight, so that the aim could be adjusted to suit the distance of the target.[21]

Men armed with crossbows were the minority, however, and much combat was hand to hand. For hand-to-hand combat, the weapon of choice was a halberd. Mounted on a long bamboo shaft, the halberd's cruel blade could be swung from a distance of up to seven and a half feet, allowing the bearer to remain out of reach of the enemy's sword. Swords—along with knives and daggers—were also in the Chinese army's arsenal; the Han Chinese were the first people anywhere to produce iron swords.

Strategy

One weapon of war wielded by the ancient Chinese was clever strategy. An example is provided in the biography of a popular general, Li Kuang, taken from *Courtier and Commoner in Ancient China: Selections from the "History of the Former Han" by Pan Ku*, by Burton Watson. Li Kuang and his posse of a hundred horsemen, in pursuit of a handful of Xiangnu hunters who had attacked a group of soldiers, spot in the distance several thousand Xiangnu on horseback.

"Li Kuang's horsemen were thoroughly terrified and begged him to flee back to camp as quickly as possible, but he replied, 'We are [about seven to ten miles] away from the main army. With only a hundred of us, if we were to make a dash for it, the [Xiangnu] would be after us in no time and would shoot down every one of us. But if we stay where we are, they are bound to think we are a decoy from the main army and will not attack.'

Instead of retreating, therefore, Li Kuang gave the order to his men to advance. When they had reached a point some [two-thirds of a mile] from the [Xiangnu] ranks, he told his men, 'Dismount and undo your saddles!'

'They expect us to run away,' said Li Kuang. 'But now if we undo our saddles and show them we have no intention of leaving, they will be more concerned than ever that there is something afoot.'"

The Xiangnu did indeed conclude that the Han military leaders had concealed soldiers in the area and were planning to attack under cover of dark. Consequently, the Xiangnu withdrew.

The strength of the iron allowed a longer sword, with the blade extending over three feet. Repeated hammering or beating of the metal at very high temperatures significantly improved the quality of the resulting steel. To increase its resistance to becoming dulled, the heated steel blade was dipped in cold water.

Spies and Other Strategies

Advances in warfare involved not only the development of weapons but also the application of strategy. Campfires were lit and then put out to deceive the enemy about an army's position, and sometimes troops pretended to appear unprepared to lull their opponents into a false sense of security. In addition, spy networks were set up to ferret out information about an enemy's tactics.

Perhaps the most significant strategic maneuver that Han military commanders used were sieges against rebellious communities within the empire as well as towns that resisted an emperor's expansionist schemes. Loewe writes about a Han assault on a Central Asian enclave in 35 B.C.:

The Han forces could see their foe displaying his many-coloured banners on the walls, at whose foot a troop of cavalry was exercising. On either side of the city gate there were infantry practising their drill in very close formation. Challenge after challenge rang out from the walls, and some hundred enemy horse [cavalryman] galloped towards the Chinese camp, to be driven off by heavy cross-bow shooting. The Han commander followed up this slight success by attacking the enemy horse [cavalryman] and foot [soldiers] that were posted outside the city, actually forcing them to withdraw inside; and the drums were now beaten for a general advance by Han troops. Each section had been allotted its sector, to ensure that all outlets from the city were blocked. The van was formed by heavy shieldsmen, and these were followed immediately by the spearmen and cross-bowmen, whose arrows forced the enemy to withdraw from the turrets and battlement of the main wall. However, there was a double palisade of wood that lay outside the fortifications, and the enemy could use this as a cover from which they could shoot at the Chinese, until the latter succeeded in setting it on fire.[22]

To help prevent their adversaries from mounting an effective siege against China's cities, Han-period military strategists pioneered the use of deterrent devices. For example, the Han Chinese were known to place numerous barbed iron balls on the ground outside their own city walls. These balls were designed so that no matter how each was placed, one sharp spike always pointed upward, deterring attacking soldiers, whether marching on foot or mounted on horses.

A Truly Great Wall

A major defensive strategy of the ancient Chinese was wall building. Not only did a wall stop the advance of an enemy, but it also offered a position of strength from which a besieged army could mount a defense. Such a strategy demonstrated an economy of force, a principle advocated in the classic Chinese manual of warfare by Sun Zi, *The Art of War*.

Probably the greatest achievement ever in defensive wall building belongs to the Chinese. Indeed, the barrier marking China's northern border has come to be known as the Great Wall. Conceived by China's first emperor as a defense against the marauding Xiangnu nomads from the north, the Qin-era wall was restored and added to by Han rulers to consolidate their eventual victory over this persistent foe. The Han also extended the wall three hundred miles westward into the Gobi Desert.

Raising a wall in the remote desert wilderness of northwest China demanded considerable ingenuity on the part of Han military engineers. Forced to use local materials, workers mixed the grit and gravel of the desert with water and then threw this mixture atop twigs of the red willow, one of the few plants tough enough to grow in the forbidding Gobi terrain. These twigs served to strengthen and stabilize the resulting wall, much like steel rods do in buildings today. Each layer of mud and twigs needed to be stamped in place for about an hour, until it became compact and its surrounding frame was ready to be removed. Built painstakingly, layer by layer, the wall absorbed the labor of hundreds of thousands of workers.

These workers toiled under punishing conditions. The weather ranged from extremes of intense heat to brutal cold—reaching thirty degrees below zero in winter. Many of those employed in wall building were convicts sentenced to hard labor, so deaths from overexertion were not a cause of concern for the wall's overseers. So many workers were hastily buried next to the wall that it has been referred to as the "Longest Graveyard in the World."[23]

On Guard

Conscripts mostly made up the garrisons along the frontier. Since other parts of the empire generally did not require a large standing force, draftees were inevitably marched off to the border. The several weeks' journey took the men from familiar, settled territory past thick, brooding forests to rugged landscapes and starkly barren stretches of land.

A rigorous, bare-bones life governed by strict discipline awaited those assigned to garrison posts. Conscripts were issued a standard uniform—tunic, trousers, socks, footwear, and defensive armor—as well as grease and glue for maintaining their weapons. Rations of grain varied depending on age and rank: Servicemen who were more advanced in rank and age were entitled to more grain. Throughout their term of service, the conscripts could expect to live and work in the watchtowers, which were built along the wall

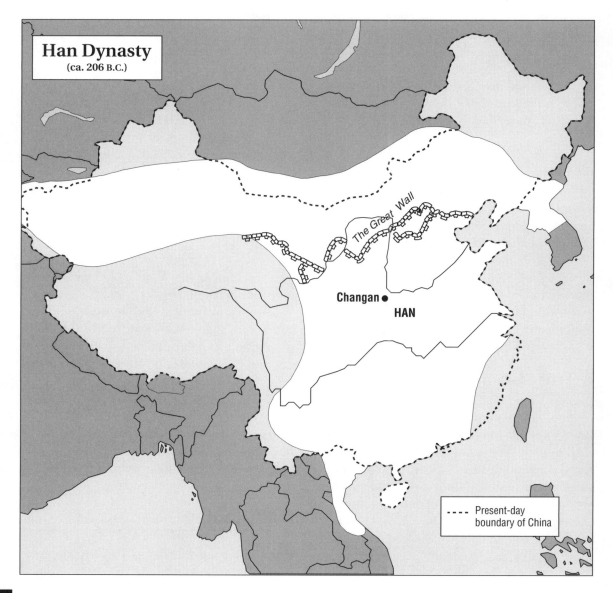

Han Dynasty
(ca. 206 B.C.)

The Great Wall

Changan •
HAN

- - - Present-day boundary of China

A remnant of an 1800-year-old Han dynasty wall, built with layers of mud and twigs. Wall-building in ancient China was painstaking work and required the labor of many men.

about every fifteen to thirty miles or so, close enough to be in sight of one another.

These towers contained several rooms each, their doors fitted with bolts to offer some security. Each tower rose to a height of up to thirty or forty feet, with a stairway or ladder leading to the top. From this elevated platform, surrounded by a parapet for protection, soldiers took turns standing on the lookout, observing enemy movement or attempts by thieves to break into the unit's store of supplies. Along with weapons—crossbows hung on the tower's walls, with quivers of arrows nearby—provisions consisted of jars of water, possibly a medicine chest with supplies of healing herbs and ointments, and food rations, including precious salt. Grain and any crops that the men managed to wrest from

the dry, resistant soil were kept in storage bins as large as 150 by 500 feet. Some conscripts stationed at the garrison labored on irrigation projects in an effort to produce food locally and thus ensure the post's self-sufficiency.

The watchtowers along the wall also served as a communications network. Messages could be sent along the ramparts with great speed, warning posts down the line, for instance, of approaching enemy troops. During the day, smoke or flags were used to send the signal; during the night, torches were used. The signal code was strictly governed by law: For example, one column of smoke indicated an attacking force of less than five hundred, two columns indicated a force of three thousand, and four columns indicated a force of up to ten thousand. Neat piles of brushwood

A watchtower along the awe-inspiring Great Wall of China. The Wall that stands today is a Ming dynasty (1368-1644) rebuilding of a much older Great Wall.

and timber, mixed with animal dung, lay stacked on the towers, ready to produce a thick column of visible black smoke when lit. Guard duties also took troops outside the wall each morning to inspect sandbanks along its north face; any disturbance in the smoothly raked sand revealed traces of an intruder, offering evidence of enemy movement.

"Peace and Prosperity"

When not on active guard duty, members of border garrisons were kept busy with a variety of tasks. Besides farming, which would have

been familiar work for many of the conscripts, some served as grooms for horses or as cooks to prepare the garrison's meals. Others might be relegated to repair or construction work on the wall or towers or else to some kind of maintenance chore, such as seeing that the pulleys used to raise flag signals were operating properly. Still others might act as couriers of official mail. Each courier was bound to a fixed schedule in a meticulously worked out relay system from one post to another.

Soldiers assigned to the Great Wall also policed China's borders, preventing the flight of criminals or deserters. Some border troops worked as customs agents, conducting searches of travelers journeying from one side of the wall to the other. Documents qualifying individuals to enter China were examined, as were any goods that travelers in either direction might be carrying, to ensure that the documents and goods were not smuggled or stolen. Detailed records were kept at border stations of the comings and goings of all people passing through the gates of the Great Wall.

During the Han dynasty, the "Ten Thousand Mile Long Wall,"[24] as it was called, followed the route of the Silk Road, a roughly defined trading route that linked China with the West, making them trading partners. Soldiers at garrisons along this trade route were ordered to protect merchants and caravans traveling nearby. They also policed the commerce that was sometimes conducted at the gates of the Great Wall. At one of these, known as the Jade Gate, marking ancient China's western frontier, a thriving market was established where not only jade but also horses, spices, gold, silks, wool, and precious stones were bought and sold. Such trade enriched those who lived near the wall. One town that grew up around a section of the wall that protected a vulnerable mountain pass proudly bore the name "Peace and Prosperity."

 In Business

Throughout the Han period, Chinese trade caravans lumbered along the trade route known as the Silk Road. Riding in wagons and on the backs of camels, merchants traveled the Silk Road's network of trails: from the capital city of Changan at its easternmost end, west across Central Asia's deserts and mountains to the edges of the Mediterranean world, and back again. Along the Silk Road's five thousand or so miles journeyed Roman glass, amber, and coral; Central Asian raisins and furs; and exotic animals like lions and rhinoceroses for the emperor's hunting parks. Westward, Chinese traders brought bronze, lacquerware, porcelain, and, of course, silk.

A caravan might not arrive at its destination with the same inventory of silks and other items that it had loaded in Changan. Merchants often swapped goods along the way, making a profit with each trade. Personnel and cargo were both replaced. Members of the support staff, including baggage handlers and professional camel drivers, were typically hired for only a stretch of the route. The result was that although some of the trade goods arriving in Changan came from Rome, those carrying the goods might well have never seen that distant city.

Traveling the Silk Road

People attaching themselves to caravans might total into the hundreds. Such numbers offered the travelers some protection, though

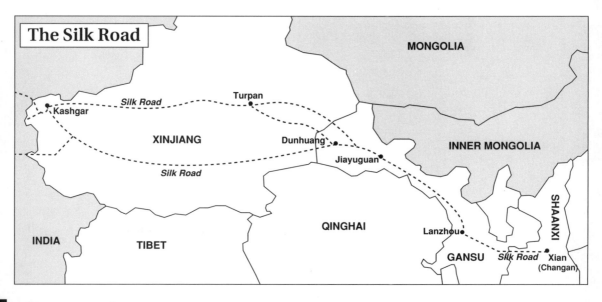

at the same time the size of both the caravan and its load forced it to move slowly, making it vulnerable to raids by roving bandits. A caravan might advance anywhere from ten or fifty miles a day, depending on the terrain. The sand dunes and rocky flats, coupled with the intense heat of the Central Asian desert, made travel arduous as well as slow. Once the caravan reached the desert, called "the Flowing Sands" by the Chinese, everyone walked, further delaying the party's progress. Pack animals, necessary for carrying supplies of food and water, were too precious to spare for the travelers' comfort. Camels generally served this purpose, for these animals could go long distances on very little nourishment. They also could smell water from far off and warn of sandstorms, during which fierce winds kicked up thick clouds of sand. As one Chinese chronicler explains,

> When such a wind is about to arrive, only the old camels have advance knowledge of it, and they immediately stand snarling together, and bury their mouths in the sand. The men always take this as a sign, and they too immediately cover their noses and mouths by wrapping them in felt. This wind moves swiftly, and passes in a moment, and is gone, but if they did not so protect themselves, they would be in danger of sudden death [by suffocation].[25]

Along the route, oasis cities such as Khotan (which lies in what is now western China) offered a welcome break from the tortuous desert journey. Safe behind the city's protective walls and enjoying fresh food provided by its irrigated fields, the party would rest and recuperate, sometimes for an entire week. These travelers also took the opportunity to replenish their supplies and perform any necessary repairs on their gear.

Punishing deserts were not the only challenges that nature posed to travelers of the Silk Road. The route wound through the Pamirs, a mountain range primarily in present-day Tajikistan that borders western China, India, and Afghanistan. The Chinese named these mountains the Tsung-Lung, meaning "Onion Mountains"—based on the mistaken notion that eating onions growing wild in the Pamirs resulted in the dizziness and nausea that travelers experienced—classic symptoms of altitude sickness caused by breathing the thin air at heights sometimes reaching twenty-five thousand feet. Adding to the travelers' discomfort, temperatures plummeted to below freezing at night, even in summertime. Worse still were the narrow mountain passes, with their treacherous sheer cliffs. Sometimes the party's pack animals had to be freed of their heavy loads and led along the steep paths while men took turns carrying the caravan's goods and supplies.

Silk and Salt

To the travelers' relief, once past the Pamirs they crossed gently sloping plateaus and broad river plains. Chinese merchants rarely traveled farther along the Silk Road than the city of Baghdad (now in Iraq), a hub of world trade in the ancient world. Most traders from China covered only one or two thousand miles of the route before turning around and heading home. Many of the bolts of silk that they had traded made their way west thanks to Arab merchants. Silk, meanwhile, became such a valuable Chinese export that the Han government took over the silk industry. The imperial regime could then closely regulate—as well as pocket profit from—its production. Government agents subsequently traveled with Silk Road caravans.

A path cuts through the ruins at Gaochang, China, once an important supply town and trading post on the Silk Road.

The Han government eventually monopolized the production of another valued commodity: salt. In a world without refrigerators, salt kept meat and vegetables from rotting. A natural source of salt was seawater, and about a dozen imperial salt plants dotted China's coast.

Inland, however, saltwater lay deep beneath the earth's surface. Workers at salt plants in China's interior labored long and hard to bring brine, or saltwater, up from depths sometimes exceeding one thousand feet. To dig a well reaching these depths with merely a drill bit, lever, and muscle power was tedious work. Only up to about three feet could be dug a day. Once the well was dug, teams of workers manually operated winding gear to draw the brine up from the earth below.

Sometimes natural gas was found along with the brine. The gas was then conveyed through bamboo pipelines to heat the furnace fueling the plant's evaporation system, which consisted of huge iron pans in which the brine was boiled away, leaving solid salt crystals behind. Workers were thus spared the exhausting work of stoking fires to heat the furnace. They were also spared the dangers of gas explosions. Recognizing the safety hazard posed by the volatility of pure natural gas, pipelines carrying the gas were directed into tanks where the gas was mixed with air before being conducted further.

Ironworks

As evidenced by the use of iron drill bits and pans in salt production, iron promoted the growth of industry in Han China. The government's desire to control this growth further motivated its takeover of the manufacture of valuable goods, including iron. Moreover, government ironworks produced items—from swords to plowshares—that helped prop up the imperial regime: Iron weapons equipped the imperial army, and iron tools helped produce the grain that fed its soldiers. In fact, the increased agricultural productivity owing to sturdy iron equipment boosted China's population significantly during the Han period.

China's population boom in turn added to its pool of workers. Along with foundries for casting, or molding, the metal (or, in the salt industry, for boiling away the brine) and pits for mining the ore (brine), Han manufacturing plants included living quarters, and these sites were practically towns. An estimated one hundred thousand men were employed each year in Han ironworks and copper plants.

While slaves worked at privately owned plants, conscripted workers and convicts labored in government industries. Forced labor, of course, could be exploited to the maximum. Fortunately for those conscripts and convicts subjected to toiling in the sweltering heat of iron and copper foundries, their terms of service—as opposed to those of slaves—ended after a definite period.

"As Bright as the Sun and Moon"

Like salt and iron, copper played an important role in people's lives in ancient China. Copper was vital to the production of bronze. Government-managed bronze factories supplied the palace as well as the army. The crossbow's precision-built trigger was produced in imperial plants. Bronze was also used to mint coins in government foundries.

Privately owned bronze factories manufactured many products used in Han homes, including pots, dishes, spoons, and incense burners. Workers in bronze also created such luxury items as mirrors. Commercial-minded owners of private workshops created their own ads for these mirrors, inscribing them right on individual pieces. "The substance of this mirror is pure and bright; the rays it radiates

Monopolies and Morality

The Han emperor Wudi established government monopolies producing iron and salt. After the emperor's death in 81 B.C., these controversial policies were debated by Confucian scholars, who questioned their morality, and by the minister who had played a part in instituting them. Their arguments are recorded in the document "Debate on Salt and Iron," excerpted here from *Chinese Civilization and Society: A Sourcebook*, edited by Patricia Buckley Ebrey.

"The Minister: The *Book of Changes* says, 'Facilitate exchange so that the people will not be overworked.' This is because . . . when valued goods are unavailable, wealth is exhausted.

The salt and iron monopolies . . . are intended to circulate accumulated wealth and to regulate consumption according to the urgency of need. It is inexpedient to abolish them.

The learned men: The government officers busy themselves with gaining control of the market and cornering commodities. With the commodities cornered, prices soar and merchants make private deals and speculate. The officers connive with the cunning merchants who are hoarding commodities against future need. Quick traders and unscrupulous officials buy when goods are cheap in order to make high profits. Where is the balance in this standard?"

could be compared to those of the sun and moon," claims one; another boasts, "The mirrors made by the Ye family are handsome and great. They are as bright as the sun and moon; indeed, they are rare to find!"[26]

Whether in privately owned or government plants, casting metal was a big job. Hundreds of workers might be involved. Once the ore was mined, a team of laborers had to haul it to the foundry. There, the ore was heated in furnaces, fed by blasts of air produced by large piston bellows. Early on in the Han dynasty, two workers operated the bellows; later, at imperial foundries, waterpower replaced manpower. After being melted down in furnaces, the hot, liquid metal was ready for casting. Workers were ordered to carry the heavy molten, or liquid, metal to the molds quickly, before it could cool and consequently harden. Workers then poured the molten bronze between a center mold and an outer mold, both made of clay. Any designs decorating the outside of the bronze item were carved on the inside of the outer mold; workers had to carve these designs backward on the mold to have them appear correctly on the finished product.

Along with workers engaged in physical labor, administrative staff members busied themselves at Han industrial plants. The chief administrator was aided by an assistant, and an executive officer made sure that the orders issued by this duo were carried out. A chief superintendent kept an eye on the plant's supervisors, who themselves managed teams of workers. Someone else saw to the inevitable paperwork.

The Merchant Class

With their complex of facilities, manufacturing sites for such consumer goods as bronze

During the Han dynasty, privately owned bronze factories produced various household items and food containers, such as the ornate bronze vessel pictured here.

The canal that runs through the modern-day city of Suzhou, China, was built in ancient times. Canal building in ancient China greatly improved water travel, shortening travel distances by as much as two-thirds or more.

utensils generally lay outside major cities. Enterprising individuals saw the opportunity to profit from directing the supply of goods from manufacturer to consumer. Their ambitions were aided by a system of overland routes linking the empire. Roads radiated out from the capital city to outlying districts like spokes from the hub of a wheel.

At the same time, water travel was improved by the building of canals. A canal connecting the capital city, Changan, with the lower Huang He, for example, shortened travel distances by two-thirds. Merchants based in Changan could sail directly up the Huang He to meet caravans arriving from the West to supply the demands of the city's many inhabitants.

Merchants in ancient China constituted a class known as the *shang*. This class included not only traders but also shopkeepers and manufacturers. Because class determined social status, a person's occupation helped form his or her identity and even sense of worth in the culture. People were evaluated in terms of how they labored on behalf of society.

Although according to this system the *nong*, or farmer class, rated higher on the social scale than the *shang* because farmers contributed needed food, the *shang* were in a position to profit from this necessity, providing

Fu-kung, or "womanly work," was touted in Han China as one of the qualities basic to femininity. Accordingly, a woman was expected to devote herself to sewing, weaving, and preparing food and drink to serve guests in her home. It was not unusual, however, for a woman who lost her husband to have to support her family.

Probably the most successful businesswoman in ancient China was a widow named Ch'ing who expertly managed her late husband's cinnabar mine in the southwest region of the country. Cinnabar, a reddish ore, or

mineral, containing a compound of mercury and sulfur, was used as a red dye. It was also valued for the magic powers it was believed to possess—the mercury it contains allows it to be turned into a silvery liquid. No doubt because of her great wealth, Ch'ing was welcomed as a guest by the emperor.

Such individuals were the exception. Most occupations were simply not open to women. Female physicians, though, were well respected. Women doctors were known to treat ladies of the imperial court.

as they did the vital link in the chain that connected farmers to consumers. On the other hand, merchants made money from the labor of others, which was considered shameful. It simply was not honest work in the view of most Chinese during the Han dynasty.

Many merchants did make fortunes by underhanded means. At harvest time, for example, they would buy up grain at very low prices and then hoard it to create shortages. Because the population—and, in the case of iron, other industries—depended on these goods, any threat to their production could wreck the economy, leading to general panic and instability. Fending off financial—and political—crisis was so important to China's emperors that they nationalized, or put under government control, the distribution of grain and other essential goods, including salt and iron.

Having his business seized did not necessarily ruin a merchant, however. To the ever-pragmatic Han regime, its subjects were above all resources to be used. That included the *shang* and their expertise. For instance, the emperor Wudi, his funds depleted from military campaigns, did not hesitate to appoint

Tung-kuo Hsien-yang, who had been a successful salt manufacturer, and K'ung Chin, who had amassed wealth from the iron trade, to assist his ministers in ensuring that the nationalized salt and iron industries turned a profit.

"Trembling Without Being Cold"

In China's carefully structured society, the extraordinary success of the *shang* brought them under scrutiny. Efforts were directed at lowering their prestige. By edict of the Han emperor Gaozu, merchants were forbidden from wearing silks, brocades, embroideries, or other fine fabrics. In addition, the privilege of carrying weapons and riding in carriages was denied them. To further hold in check their power and influence, the *shang* were prohibited from holding office in the government bureaucracy.

Han emperors also actively pursued policies aimed at separating the *shang* from their wealth. Heavy taxes were levied on their property as well as on their carts and boats.

For neglecting to properly report their wealth, their property could be confiscated. During the reign of Wudi, a total of 10 million slaves owned by merchants were seized because the merchants' financial accounts failed to meet the dictates of the law.

The imperial government could and often did meddle in the affairs of the *shang,* although they put up no barriers to joining the merchant class. Anyone with money to invest in goods could hope to increase his wealth, although doing so might be distasteful. Reflecting on his need to make a living, a dismissed official named Yan Yün wrote in a letter to a friend,

Fortunately, I have [some] savings from my official salary and am buying at low prices and selling at high prices, thereby pursuing the way of one-tenth profit. These are the activities of worthless merchants and a vile and humiliating position, but I personally practice it. One who is a man of low standing, where all defamations will flow in upon him, is trembling without being cold.[27]

To rein in their ambitions, the *shang* were generally allowed access to only a limited list of commodities. Most merchants were forced to content themselves with peddling humble products such as bamboo poles, ox carts, brass utensils, and woven mats. Despite such restrictions, some entrepreneurs still managed to amass fortunes. A sauce merchant, for

A Han statuette of a fish merchant from the shang *class. The* shang *were not highly regarded in ancient China because it was considered shameful to make money from the labor of others.*

example, built an estate valued at 10 million copper coins.

As in any society, moneylending also offered an opportunity to earn a hefty income. In 154 B.C., when the emperor desperately needed funds to quell a rebellion, an individual able to supply a lot of cash quickly ended up earning in interest ten times the amount he lent. Despite the low regard that society held them in, wealthy *shang* occasionally associated with nobles and officials—when it was in these esteemed individuals' interest, of course. Money had a way of breaking down some, if not all, barriers in Han China.

Put in Pens

At the bottom of the Han social scale were slaves. This class, known as the *nu*, remained relatively small, totaling less than 5 percent of the population. While some were slaves since birth, their parents being themselves enslaved, a large number of Chinese found themselves suddenly stripped of their freedom for various reasons. In addition to the farm children who were sold by their parents in order to pay debts, prisoners of war faced enslavement. Also tribal peoples living along the empire's western border would occasionally provide human prisoners as bribes to imperial officials who then ignored smuggling attempts. Regardless of the reason, the faces of those whose freedom was taken from them might be tattooed, marking them as slaves for the rest of their lives.

Slaves were sold in the market like cattle and horses—after being adorned to catch the attention of buyers. "Nowadays," reads a document from Han times, "when people sell their slaves, they dress them up in embroidered clothes and silk shoes with braided trimmings on the edges, and put them in pens."[28]

The Han-era Chinese assigned their slaves a wide variety of tasks. Slaves owned by merchants labored not only in their masters' homes but also in their businesses. They worked, for example, in fisheries and in plants producing charcoal. Seven hundred slaves were taught by the wife of one estate owner to spin and weave, contributing to the family's cloth industry. Male slaves who seemed particularly capable were sometimes trained to perform clerical duties. The lifetime service required of such slaves made this instruction a good investment for the slave owners.

While the majority of *nu* were slaves for life, some did win their freedom. For instance, a devoted slave whose age made him too feeble to render even routine service was sometimes freed. A female servant who became her master's concubine, or secondary wife, was no longer considered a slave. Such a slave could occasionally rise to dizzying heights. Wei Tzu-fu, the daughter of a slave who served a princess, was elevated to the status of imperial concubine by Emperor Wu and was later selected to be empress.

Some More Equal than Others

A slave was under the complete control of his or her master. A master had the right to beat a slave whom he judged to be disobedient. However, Han law did not excuse a master who killed a slave, though punishment for killing or injuring a slave was less severe than if the victim were a free person. A slave was simply not seen as a free person's equal in the eyes of the law.

Despite their overall low status, not all slaves were equal. Their ranking within the *nu* class depended on the kind of work they did. Slaves laboring in private copper mines, with their shaved heads and iron collars, had

A Han dynasty bronze sculpture of a man, perhaps a slave, holding an umbrella. Slaves, in a class known as the nu, *were at the bottom of the Han social scale.*

an inferior status to those who served as their masters' bodyguards and were allowed to dress in silks.

In general, the status of slaves was determined by that of their masters; slaves of influential masters sometimes associated with government officials and rode with them in their carriages. During the Han dynasty, earlier prohibitions against slaves mixing with their masters and their families were relaxed. In fact, one nobleman became so friendly with his male slaves that they joined him in drinking parties.

A Class with "Class"

Rated higher socially than the *nu* and the *shang*, though below the *nong*, were members of the *gong*, or artisan class. Like the *nong*, the *gong* were perceived as productive members of society—as opposed to the exploitative and acquisitive *shang*—although what they produced was not considered essential, as food was. Less well off economically than the merchants who sold their handiwork, the *gong* could, unlike the *shang*, be appointed to official posts and therefore

Items like this beautifully carved, decorative jade scabbard from the early Han dynasty were created by members of the gong, *or artisan class.*

enjoyed greater social mobility. One highly admired painter, for example, was offered positions in both the central and local governments of the Han regime.

The *gong* were skilled in such crafts as carving jewels and other precious stones. They also designed the molds for casting iron and bronze. In addition, the *gong* created elaborate patterns for silks and brocades, varying from zigzagging bands enclosing dragons or phoenixes to curvy forms described as cloud scroll. They also made the punched cards that served as a sort of primitive program for looms to produce letters directly on fabrics, spelling out prayers for "ten thousand lifetimes, and all you wish" or "long life, with a goodly blessing of sons and grandsons."[29]

As the technicians of Han society, the skills of the *gong* were valued in times of peace and war. They produced weapons as elegant in their design as they were deadly in their effect. They also created luxury items whose beauty and sophistication raised them to the level of art.

With Artistry

The prosperity ushered in by the Han dynasty encouraged the flourishing of craftsmanship and the arts. The patronage of the emperor, imitated by wealthy families eager to appear fashionable, supported the crafting of exquisite works by Chinese artisans. Throughout the Han era, the decorative arts continued to serve practical ends, from beautifying objects handled by the privileged classes to adorning vessels used in ceremonial feasts. At the same time, a greater freedom and expressiveness was evident in the work of the *gong*.

Part of this development was due to the passing of the repressive Qin regime, which released the *gong* from the rigors of a fixed, formal style to experiment with a more naturalistic one. Further encouraging this change was the growth of a leisured, moneyed class eager to purchase practical objects that were artistically rendered. Thus, a bronze lamp might be shaped like a bird or an incense burner formed in the likeness of a mountain inhabited by wild animals. The desire to continue enjoying earthly pleasures, even into death, shows in the toylike figures of dancers and musicians and horse-led carriages occupying Han-era tombs. In one such tomb, a particularly lifelike bronze galloping horse is posed with a bird underneath one of its hooves.

Sculptures of dancers, musicians, and jugglers, like these found in Han-era tombs, are evidence of the Han people's desire to continue enjoying earthly pleasures even after death.

Meanwhile, the pleasing sense of symmetry and balance characterizing the work of the *gong* derived from the high value the Chinese placed on harmony. Decoration is rarely crowded or jumbled but is instead symmetrical and proportionate. The aim of Han artists

A decorative bronze mirror from the Han dynasty. The Han believed that such mirrors possessed magic powers.

and artisans was to appeal to the moral, visual, and tactile senses. The beauty of the natural world was believed to express the ordered perfection of the universe, which humans must strive to emulate in their own lives. The loveliness of the objects the Han Chinese surrounded themselves with thus invited contemplation as well as reflection on one's relationship with the cosmos.

Magic Mirrors

As a vehicle for self-reflection, the bronze mirror was among the most distinctive crafts of the Han era. One side of the mirror was smoothed and polished until it shone. Its glossy surface allowed the user to study his or her reflection. On the other side the artisan might improvise on the familiar grass-leaf or star-cloud pattern inspired by nature.

Often the *gong* illustrated the backs of bronze mirrors with a circular universe enclosing a square Earth. T-shapes at the sides of the square signified the sacred mountains supporting the heavens. The four directions were represented by their guardian animals: a bird for the south, a tiger for the west, a dragon for the east, and a tortoise, often intertwined with a snake, for the north. As suggested by such potent mythic imagery, Han bronze mirrors were believed to possess magic powers. Many a person wore one suspended on a cord from his or her waist as a protection against evil spirits.

Cutting-Edge Craftsmanship

Lacquerware as well as bronze design also achieved a high degree of artistry in the Han. The durable quality of lacquer—the sap from the lac, a kind of oak tree—made it an excel-

Lacquerware

As evidence of its value, a piece of lacquerware was often inscribed with details of its manufacture. Identified were the year of manufacture, the particular workshop, and the team of laborers and supervisors responsible for its production. Different personnel were involved in different stages of producing the piece.

One worker formed the wood or fabric core. Other workers applied the lacquer: One applied the base coat, another the top coat. Some other worker attached any metal parts to the piece, such as the handles on a tray. Another worker painted surface designs. Still another polished and buffed the lacquered surface until it shone. A product inspector ensured that the piece was up to standard. Finally, a supervisor checked off on it.

Intricately painted lacquerware cosmetic boxes from the Han dynasty.

lent material for boxes, bowls, and other products used daily. Sword sheaths and shields were also coated with this tough preservative, as were coffins.

In addition, lacquer's hard finish served as an ideal surface for the engraver or painter. Sometimes the engraver incised, or cut, a decoration into the lacquered surface with a pointed tool resembling a needle. These incised designs might then be filled with some glittery material like gold, silver, or tortoise shell. An artist painting the lacquerware surface selected from a palette of colors, including red, green, yellow, and blue. Most painters favored a delicate, flowing style to convey designs inspired by nature: birds, fish, flowers, or a scrolling cloud image. A brush was evidently used to achieve this style.

Jade was another material displaying the artistry of the *gong*. Intricate designs appear incised on the stone's surface. Valued at times more highly than silver and gold, jade was associated by the ancient Chinese with immortality because of its seeming indestructibility. Indeed, jade was so hard a material that until the development of iron tools during the Han dynasty, the *gong* had to apply sand as an abrasive to a tool's cutting edge to grind away the stone. With the advent of iron tools, artisans could hollow out bowls and even carve three-dimensional figures. Making the most of the new opportunities for artistic expression, Han artisans carved jade figures of deer and dragons in stunning detail.

The moral qualities that the Chinese invested in jade are noted in this ancient dictionary definition:

> Jade is the fairest of stones. It is endowed with five virtues. Charity is typified by its lustre, bright yet warm; rectitude by its translucency, revealing the colour and markings within; wisdom by the purity and penetrating quality of its note, when the stone is struck; courage in that it may be broken but cannot be bent; equity in that it has sharp angles which yet injure none.[30]

A Cheaper, Better Writing Material

A material ultimately more valuable than jade was invented in Han China, and that was paper. The inventor is said to have been a court official named Cai Lun. Apparently sometime in the first century A.D. Cai Lun saw the possibilities in a silk wash rag that was being wrung out to dry. He experimented with recycling the fraying silk fibers to create a smooth writing surface. Later, plants like hemp, bamboo, straw, the trunk of the mulberry tree, and even seaweed were used to produce paper.

Before the use of Cai Lun's invention, people wrote on expensive silks. Such material could easily be rolled into scrolls, but its high cost limited its use. Silk's expense may well have inspired a budget-conscious court bureaucrat such as Cai Lun to experiment with its waste fibers. In any event, once paper replaced silk for producing longer written works, sheets were glued together and then similarly wound up into a scroll. Paper thus offered a new, more affordable medium of communication for the government bureaucrat as well as the scholar and poet.

An alternative to costly silk did exist before paper. Bamboo was cheap and plentiful, so strips of it were commonly written on. The Chinese wrote their word symbols vertically, one after the other, in columns lining up and down the slender reeds of bamboo. A book was produced by tying a series of bamboo strips, covered on one side with writing, together in a bundle. But bamboo had disadvantages of its own. Such bundles were bulkier than delicate silk scrolls. Not only did they take up a lot of space, but they were also awkward to use. Lighter and more flexible, paper was a welcome improvement.

Whether on bamboo, silk, or paper, writing in ancient China was done with ink and a brush. Finely powdered soot, generally from burned pine trees and other plants, produced the black pigment of the ink. This was mixed with glue and formed into a stick or block. Sometimes, instead of a square block, the mixture was molded into the shape of a dragon or mythological bird.

When ready to write, scribes ground the solid ink mass into a few drops of water on an inkstone. This slab of stone or pottery provided a firm, even surface for finely grinding the mass. First-rate, smoothly flowing ink was the result.

The ink was applied on the writing surface with a brush. The brush generally had a bamboo handle. Deer hair made up the brush itself. A scribe could choose from a variety of types of brushes, depending on his purpose. For writing large on banners, for example, brushes with hairs over a foot long were available. The scribe "erased" any mistakes by scraping the ink away with a knife.

Becoming a scribe in ancient China took years of study and practice. For one thing, an aspiring scribe had to master proper posture. The brush needed to be held upright, and elbows were never allowed to rest on the table.

"Word Pictures"

Many of the tools and techniques used by skilled Han scribes were the same as those used by painters. In fact, the expressiveness of the scribes' work transformed writing into art. That art, known as calligraphy, has been practiced in China ever since.

With brush and ink, ancient Chinese calligraphers could create an impressive variety of lines, from delicate to bold. Writing—and consequently reading—was for the ancient

An illustration of early Chinese papermaking. Invented in Han China, paper provided a better, more affordable writing surface than silk.

The Dragon

The figure of a dragon—with its head of a camel, horns of a deer, scales of a fish, claws of an eagle, ears of a bull, and whiskers of a cat—often appeared as decoration on fabrics and luxury items such as mirrors. The Chinese dragon, however, was not considered a fearsome figure. Instead, its presence on a piece of clothing or household item evoked positive images.

Dragons symbolized wisdom, goodness, and strength for the ancient Chinese. Winged dragons transported a person from this world into a life of immortal bliss. Representing the life-giving power of water, dragons were believed to live high among the rain clouds as well as in rivers, lakes, and oceans.

The figure of a dragon adorns a Chinese wall. In ancient China, the dragon symbolized goodness, wisdom, and strength.

Chinese a sensual as well as intellectual experience. The ideal was a rapid, seemingly spontaneously executed brush stroke, suggesting movement and vitality. Taken together on the page, the individual strokes, varying in thickness, conveyed a three-dimensional quality in an image. Every stroke derived its inspiration from a natural object. Chinese calligraphers reported closely studying natural phenomena: the graceful movements of the necks of geese, for instance, or clouds wafted by the summer wind.

Helping advance the art of calligraphy in China was the pictorial quality of Chinese writing. Instead of an alphabet in which letters represent sounds, the Chinese used pictograms, or stylized pictures, each signifying a word. Sometimes pictograms were combined to form new meanings. For example, two or three pictograms for a tree placed together signified a forest. One tradition traces the inspiration for written characters to the markings on the back of a mythical turtle that emerged from the Huang He. When writing was invented, legend says, "all spirits cried in agony, as the innermost secrets of nature were thus revealed."[31]

Poetic Inspiration

Whether the characters of Chinese writing literally reveal nature's secrets, nature is a vital presence in much of Chinese poetry. Chinese poets have often used images from the natural world to set mood. Feelings and emotions are frequently conveyed through natural phenomena, such as joy represented by a bubbling spring.

A major theme in Chinese poetry, powerfully evoked through nature imagery, was and continues to be the impermanence of human life and relationships. These verses, written during the Han and translated by scholar Arthur Waley, offer an example:

> The bright moon, oh how white it
>   shines,
> Shines down on the gauze curtains of my
>   bed!
> Racked by sorrow I toss and cannot
>   sleep;
> Picking up my clothes, I wander up and
>   down,
> My absent love says that he is happy,
> But I would rather he said he was
>   coming back.
> Out in the courtyard I stand hesitating,
>   alone;
> To whom can I tell the sad thoughts I
>   think?
> Staring before me I enter my room
>   again;
> Falling tears wet my mantle and robe.[32]

Poetic Landscape

The following verse from "Fu on the Shang-lin Park," by the second-century B.C. poet Szu-ma Hsiang-ju, is typical of Chinese poetry's ability to convey a vivid image in just a few words. The poem is found in *Ancient China*, by Edward H. Schafer and the editors of Time-Life Books.

> "The steep summit of the Nine
>   Pikes,
> The towering heights of the
>   Southern Mountains,
> Soar dizzily like a stack of cooking
>   pots,
> Precipitous and sheer."

Highly revered in Han China was the *Shijing,* or *Book of Poetry.* Confucian editors, intent on assigning the *Shijing* an educational role in Chinese life, evidently altered to some degree the original ritual hymns and chants as well as the odes to powerful lords and the folk rhymes collected in this work from earlier times. The preface to the *Shijing,* prepared by these editors, claims, "The ancient kings used [the poems in the collection] to regulate the tie between husband and wife, to perfect filial piety and respectfulness, to beautify moral instruction, and to transform the customs of the people."[33] Such moralizing aside, the strong lyrical appeal of what were initially popular songs remains. Indeed, the poems in the *Shijing* set the pattern for poetry in the Han and later periods. Features of Chinese poetry such as a strict rhythmic pattern and an emphasis on imagery can be traced to the *Shijing.*

Personal Histories

The same instructive purpose attributed to the *Shijing* lay behind the great works of Chinese historical writing. The deep concern with history in China was allied with ancestor worship and the need to record family deeds and events worthy of honor and celebration. In addition, Han China's guiding philosopher, Confucius, regarded history as a kind of mirror in which later generations could view themselves and judge their own behavior.

Epitomizing this tradition is the *Records of the Historian,* or the *Shiji,* which was produced during the Han period and provides readers with numerous models of virtuous or evil conduct to follow or avoid. A truly ambitious work containing a total of 130 chapters, the *Shiji* intended to cover the whole of human history, at least as the Chinese understood it, from its beginnings to the author's

Ming dynasty portrayal of a rugged Chinese landscape. In similar fashion, Han-era Chinese poetry drew heavily on images of nature to set mood.

death in 90 B.C. The *Shiji's* author, Sima Qian, was appointed to the post of grand historian of the Han in 107 B.C. and began writing a few years later. His official post helped him research his book, allowing him to hunt through the documents of the imperial library, consult the contents of private libraries, and interview scholars and the elderly for their perspectives on events. The result is far from a dry, impersonal document.

Sima Qian approached the writing of history with a definite point of view. According to this view, Chinese dynastic history revealed a pattern, and that pattern had a lesson to teach. Invariably in the *Shiji,* a promising start by a brave and virtuous leader deteriorates after a number of generations into tyranny. The cycle is repeated when a new heroic leader overthrows a corrupt ruler and sets up a new dynasty. Subsequent historians continued to trace this pattern in future dynasties.

Such an approach to history casts historical figures into the dramatic roles of heroes and villains. Not surprisingly, richly detailed biographies of generals, politicians, philosophers, and other figures influential at court make up the bulk of the *Shiji.* This is also true of the *Han Shu,* or *History of the Former Han,* written by Pan Ku in the first century A.D. Like the *Shiji,* the *Han Shu* offers a moral interpretation of the historical events it relates. The ancient Chinese believed that human misrule could disrupt nature, resulting in strange weather and other phenomena. In his history, Pan Ku records such phenomena and finds that they are caused by improper behavior by those in power. Serving as cautionary literature, such histories as the *Shiji* and the *Han Shu* at the same time filled a place in ancient Chinese life similar to novels (once they appeared several hundred years later), as their writers' gifts as storytellers captured readers' imaginations.

A Court Jester

In Burton Watson's *Courtier and Commoner in Ancient China: Selections from the "History of the Former Han" by Pan Ku,* Tung-Fang Shuo, a favorite at the court of the Emperor Wu, is characterized by Pan Ku as "a man of jests and witticisms, an actor and a buffoon." As evidence of his brashness and quick wit, one summer Tung-Fang Shuo "took it upon himself to draw his sword and cut off a portion of meat, saying to fellow officials, 'In these hot days one ought to go home early. With your permission, therefore, I will take my gift.' Then he put the meat into the breast of his robe and went off."

The imperial butler dutifully reported the jester's behavior to the emperor. When Tung-Fang Shuo again appeared at court, the emperor directed him to "confess" his "faults." Pan Ku relates the episode.

"Shuo bowed twice and said, 'All right now, Shuo! You accepted the gift without waiting for the imperial command—what a breech of etiquette! You drew your sword and cut the meat—what singular daring! When you carved it up, you didn't take much—how [frugal] of you! You took it home and gave it to the little lady—how big-hearted!'

The emperor laughed and said, 'I told you to confess your faults and here you are praising yourself!' Then he presented him with a further gift of a gallon of wine and [133 pounds] of meat."

Serving the Need for Entertainment

While the narrative gifts of historians such as Sima Qian and Pan Ku effectively balanced their moral impulses, keeping their work from descending into propaganda, some artistic efforts in Han China made no claim whatsoever to moral instruction. Numerous skilled performers offered their audiences pure escapism. At sumptuous feasts, singers, dancers, jugglers, and performers adept at sword play and acrobatic feats amused wealthy hosts and their guests. Dancing girls wore beautifully embroidered robes with sleeves that extended beyond their hands and swirled gracefully with the dancer's movements.

A number of wealthy households had their own troupes of entertainers. Dancing and singing professionally required many years of training, so instruction was intensive and began at an early age. Teachers often arranged with poor families to take young girls off their hands and raise them to be entertainers. The girls were then sold as slaves to perform for rich families.

Sometimes the performing arts served their practitioners well. Attractive singing and dancing girls occasionally caught the eye of a master, and these individuals moved up the social ladder to become concubines. One Han empress started out in life as a dancer, another as a singer.

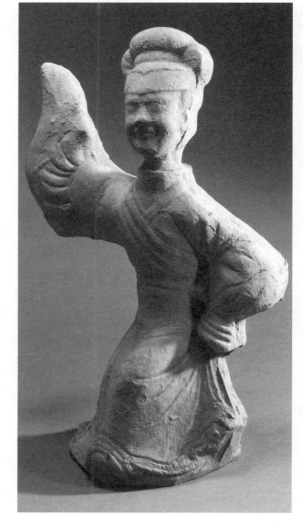

A Han sculpture of a female dancer. Becoming a professional dancer required years of training, so most dancers began their training at a young age.

Music's Mysteries

Wealthy Chinese households during the Han not only had their own troupes of performers but also their own five-piece orchestras. Wind, string, and percussion instruments were all represented in Han-era ensembles. The *sheng*, an instrument that resembled a mouth organ and was made of bamboo pipes, served as the wind section. Mastery of this instrument required dexterity and coordination, as the player fingered holes in the pipes while alternately blowing air into and sucking air out of them. In the orchestras of ancient China, several *sheng* were played together.

The *qin*, meanwhile, was a kind of long-bodied zither. Players plucked its strings by hand to produce a sound that induced pensiveness in listeners. Han orchestras also included triangular chimes made of limestone. Hanging in sets from racks and struck by mallets, these chimes could play complex, sophisticated melodies. Other percussion instruments included stone drums, gongs, and bells. Having no clappers inside them, Chinese bells produced a tone by being struck on the outside.

The ancient Chinese classified their musical instruments by the material used to make them. These materials included bamboo, wood, stone, clay, metal, skin, and silk. The bodies of some instruments were made from hollowed-out gourds. Each instrument was associated musically with a season and some feature of nature. The *sheng*, for example, was associated with spring and with mountains; bronze bells were linked with autumn and the quality of dampness.

As suggested by such symbolic associations, the ancient Chinese believed that music possessed mystical as well as moral powers. Sound, they were convinced, affected the harmony of the universe. The distances that music traveled, they reasoned, crossed the borders between the visible and invisible, or earthly and heavenly, worlds. Music could convey messages between those worlds.

A bureau of the Han government was devoted to monitoring the music used in ceremonies, and hundreds of musicians were employed at the imperial palace. Confucius had taught that music could dispel the "passions" that led people to behave aggressively. Music, therefore, could be morally uplifting and ultimately purifying; music produced by the *qin* was thought to be particularly conducive to meditation. In the Confucian view, no moral education was complete without the study of music.

In Harmony

Whether attempting to flow with nature according to Daoist philosophy, harmonize one's relationships with others as prescribed by Confucian teachings, or reach a blissful state by liberating oneself from desire through Buddhist practices, the ancient Chinese grappled with reconciling the twin mysteries of life and death. Known as "the Three Ways," Daoism, Confucianism, and Buddhism coexisted peacefully in Han China. As a result, persecution for one's beliefs was virtually unknown among the Chinese of ancient times.

Compared with Daoism and Confucianism, Buddhism was a relative newcomer to China, having reached China from India by way of trade routes. Nevertheless, once Buddhist teachings came to the attention of the imperial court, sometime in the first century A.D., the emperor was sufficiently impressed to send ambassadors to India. The ambassadors' mission was to bring back copies of the sutras, or Buddhist holy books, along with scholars to translate and help interpret these texts. The hope Buddhism offered for freeing the body and soul from pain in the living world eventually won great acceptance in China.

Meanwhile, Daoism's mystical tendencies and Confucianism's focus on social relationships offered a spiritual balance for most Chinese of the Han period. Moreover, these major philosophical currents flowed smoothly into the great stream of beliefs and practices that the majority of China's people had engaged in for centuries.

The Spirit World

Underlying the practice of the Three Ways was a belief in spirits animating the natural world, particularly among the *nong*. These spirits were envisioned in bodily form. For ex-

A Han dynasty bronze sculpture representing Feather Man, one of a number of mythical beings depicted in ancient Chinese art.

ample, Fei-lien, a kind of bird with a deer's head, made the wind blow, and Lei-shih, also known as Feng-lung, a dragon with the head of a man, beat its stomach or, alternatively, tapped a drum to produce thunder.

The supreme being, known as Shangdi, ruled the spirit world and exercised ultimate authority over the lives of human beings. It was Shangdi, for example, who determined whether an emperor suffered an illness or won a victory on the battlefield. Shangdi's palace, located at the center of heaven, was guarded by the celestial Wolf, known in the West as the star Sirius. Thronging Shangdi's court were the gods of the sun, moon, wind, rain, and thunder, as well as the Five Lords, one for each direction: north, south, east, west, and center. (The lord of the center governed the center of the world—that is, China.) Life at Shangdi's court, just like at the Han emperor's, was filled with feasting and musical entertainment. Shangdi's administration also resembled that of the emperor in its proliferation of heavenly deputies and assistants. Jo-shou, for example, functioned as Shangdi's minister of punishments and Kou-mang as his minister of rewards.

Corresponding to the hierarchy evident in Shangdi's heavenly court, the Great God of the Soil had his own subordinates: the local gods of the soil. To ensure the fertility of the soil in his particular domain, the god's favor was sought with ritual beating of drums as well as sacrifices. A fierce god believed to crave blood, the Great God of the Soil was depicted as a monster with an ox's body and a tiger's head, having horns and three eyes.

Most alarming were the evil spirits who preyed on human beings. These included the *wang-laing*, or echoes, who were envisioned as long-haired children who imitated travelers' voices to lead them astray, and demons, who caused epidemics, baring their tiger fangs. Malevolent spirits were also believed to threaten human beings with natural disasters; for example, droughts were considered the work of the ill-tempered Lady Pi.

Ritual Acts

When riled, these forces could wreak havoc on human life and property. To help maintain public order, the imperial government took the lead in conducting rites to appease powerful natural phenomena. For instance, once when the Huang He showed signs of flooding its banks, the provincial governor personally approached the riverbank, with his underlings tagging along behind. A gray horse was thrown into the current as an offering to the river god; meanwhile the governor, clutching jade objects believed to possess magical powers, ordered the attendant priests to recite the appropriate prayers. Undeterred, the level of the water continued to rise. One by one, the local people fled, leaving the official to stand alone with a single assistant to face the raging god. Eventually the governor was rewarded, first by the leveling off of the floodwaters and second by an imperial edict praising him for his steadfastness and granting him a promotion.

Generally, prayer and ritual were engaged in for the benefit of the community rather than the individual. People in Han China experienced worship mostly as a public, official activity. Ritual, for example, was believed to help along the orderly progress of the agricultural seasons. Consequently, a series of ritual celebrations, in the form of festivals, accompanied the change of seasons. The life endured by the *nong*—shifting between laboring in the fields and shutting themselves up in their huts to wait out the winter—was elevated by these festivals into a ritual act.

As a kind of demigod linking the earthly and heavenly realms, the emperor led the way in ceremonies central to the seasonal festivals. For instance, at the appropriate time—determined by the imperial diviners—the emperor performed the plowing ceremony that lifted the ban on working the land. Guiding the plow with his own hand, he symbolically tilled the sacred field lying south of the capital by turning up a single chunk of soil. With this action, he launched the season of sowing and planting.

Marking the end of the growing season was the Grand Festival in Honor of the Spirits Who Are to Be Sought Out. This festival celebrated the spirits who had protected the season's crops from natural disasters and predators. Those honored included the spirits of cats, which killed rats, and tigers, which attacked the wild boars that sometimes invaded farmers' fields. To pay them tribute, adults as well as children masqueraded as cats and tigers during the celebration.

Priests and Shamans

While the emperor served as his people's sacred representative in the heavenly court, performing pivotal seasonal sacrifices and ritual acts, communication between the world of human beings and the realm of gods and spirits routinely happened through the mediation of priests and shamans. Priests belonged

A Chinese sacrifice to the harvest moon. During Han times, worship and ritual celebrations were public activities, believed to assist the changing of seasons.

to the same class as government officials. As with all other government personnel in Han China, priests functioned as part of a bureaucracy. Each priest learned the formulas and practices for officiating at a particular activity; for example, there was a priest of the hunt.

Other than demonstrating knowledge of official rites, priests underwent no initiation ceremony. Shamans, however, demonstrated their selection by the spirits who possessed them in often dramatic ways, such as remaining in a trance for extended periods. Having come by their profession by such unorthodox means, shamans played a minor role in official worship, especially in urban areas. They might be called on during a sacrifice, for instance, to conjure up a spirit with an incantation.

Shamans, however, played a much greater role in the religious life of China's peasants. Known as *wu*, or sorcerers, shamans conducted healing and purifying ceremonies for the *nong*. Female shamans generally performed purification rites as well as ritual dances to improve growing conditions, such as ending a drought. It was believed that their drops of sweat, produced by exerting themselves while dancing in the hot sun, had the power to coax rain from the heavens.

The Healing Art

The *nong* also turned to shamans for combating disease, but physicians did treat patients who had access to their professional services. Han-era doctors conducted medical exams, kept records on patients, and wrote out prescriptions for their treatment. A fragment of a prescription found at the site of a military garrison lists as ingredients various herbs:

For feverish colds, four ingredients:
Wu hui   10 parts
Chü   10 parts
Hsi hsin   6 parts
Kuei   4 parts
One dose to be taken in hot water three times daily and twice nightly.[34]

Drugs were used either as an alternative to or along with acupuncture in treating illness. Acupuncture involves the use of silver, brass, or other metal needles of different lengths and thicknesses. To relieve pain, a treatment known as *moxibustion* was sometimes prescribed in combination with acupuncture. *Moxibustion* involved fitting acupuncture needles with caps; in these caps the dried herb *mugwort* was burned. The needles then served to transfer pain-reducing heat to the body.

Acupuncture was, and remains today, an important part of Chinese medicine. Needles were carefully inserted at points where the *qi*, or life energy of the body, was understood to flow. This process released the forces of yin and yang acting adversely on the patient. The basis of traditional Chinese medicine lay in balancing these contrasting energies in the human body.

Yin and Yang

People in ancient China viewed life and the universe as the product of the interacting forces known as yin and yang. *Yin* literally means "shaded" and *yang* "sunlit." *Yin* stands for the dark, cool, wet, and yielding aspects of nature; *yang* represents the qualities considered bright, warm, and aggressive. All attempts were made to harmonize human activity with the interplay of these energies. Edward H. Schafer and the editors of Time-Life Books explain the role of yin and yang in the change of seasons and in rituals accompanying this change:

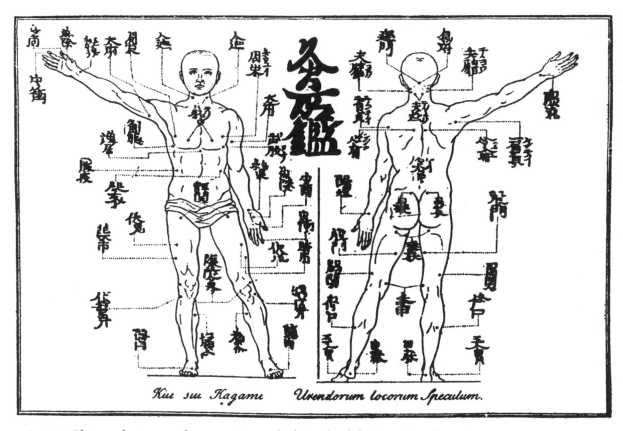

Kiu su Kagami   Urendorum locorum Speculum.

Ancient Chinese doctors used acupuncture, which involved the insertion of metal needles at precise pressure points on the body noted in this diagram, to treat illness and relieve pain.

The *yin* power reached its climax in the world at the time of the winter solstice. Then the Son of Heaven made the greatest of all sacrifices, the sacrifice to Heaven . . . and brought back the warm celestial force of *yang* to draw the new crops out of the wet soil. The *yang* force reached its own maximum in midsummer and then began to decline, yielding to the power of *yin*.[35]

Eventually all aspects of life were categorized by the ancient Chinese as either yin or yang and dealt with accordingly. Veterinarians, for example, geared their treatment to whether an animal was yin or yang—a determination based on whether an animal rose to a standing position by first using its front legs or its hind ones. Yin animals, which lifted their hind end, included camels; horses were considered yang because they lifted their front legs.

The ancient Chinese believed that all natural processes flowed from the interaction of yin and yang with the elements of the material world. Considered dynamic rather than static and inert, these elements were known as the five activities or five phases. They included fire, water, earth, metal, and wood. The five elements became associated with the five senses as well as the five fingers of the hand and five toes of the foot. Each element was also linked with a particular number and color.

Much of the protocol at court was an effort to claim a particular element as guardian of the dynasty in power, thus lending legitimacy to the dynasty's rule. The Han dynasty, for instance, justified its rule as embodying the element of earth, and the appropriate color, yellow, was ceremonially displayed at court. Earth was adopted as the Han dynasty's element because, according to the succession of the five phases evident in nature, it was able to soak up and therefore overcome the element of water that had been adopted by the preceding Qin dynasty.

The *Book of Changes*

The interplay of yin and yang and the five elements was complex and required interpretation. Interpreting the interplay of these phenomena, which was displayed in unusual occurrences in nature, was the job of the diviner. Diviners read omens in rainbows, for example, and also in meteor showers and in haloes around the moon. Because they were supposed to be able to warn of future disasters, the skills of diviners were in demand at the imperial court.

Divination was also done by throwing down sticks and interpreting the resulting configuration of lines. A book produced during the Han dynasty, called the *I Ching,* or *Book of Changes,* was consulted to determine which of sixty-four symbolic forms matched the pattern of the thrown sticks.

The editors who produced the *Book of Changes* compiled keys to interpreting the symbolic forms, known as hexagrams, or figures having six lines. The symbolic significance of each form was presented in terse, enigmatic passages and was elaborated on in philosophical commentary. The *Book of Changes* was called on to determine the "truth" in all kinds of situations, from earthquakes to suspicions of unfaithfulness in a marriage.

Immortality

Other practitioners of the occult arts concerned themselves with fulfilling the desire

Health as Harmony

The Yellow Emperor's Classic of Medicine, the basic medical text of ancient China, was likely put in final form during the Han period. An excerpt from *Chinese Civilization and Society: A Sourcebook,* edited by Patricia Buckley Ebrey, shows the impact of the concepts of yin and yang on the medical arts.

"When Yang is the stronger, the body is hot, . . . and people begin to pant; they . . . do not perspire. They become feverish, their mouths are dry and sore, their stomachs feel tight, and they die of constipation. . . . When Yin is the stronger, the body is cold and covered with perspiration. People . . . tremble and feel chilly. . . . Their stomachs can no longer digest food and they die.

Experts in examining patients judge their general appearance; they feel their pulse and determine whether it is Yin or Yang that causes the disease. . . . To determine whether Yin or Yang predominates, one must be able to distinguish a light pulse of low tension from a hard, pounding one. With a disease of Yang, Yin predominates. With a disease of Yin, Yang predominates. When one is filled with vigor and strength, Yin and Yang are in proper harmony."

for immortality. The longing for continued existence in one's own body, free of deterioration, was common. Others envisioned the bliss of never-ending life in a different world altogether. In either case, experts were relied on to help achieve an immortal existence.

Such "experts" presented themselves as masters of the occult, known as the *fang-shih*. They claimed to have access to magic potions or practices able to preserve the body indefinitely. Elixirs made of such exotic ingredients as ground-up pearls and gold were given to those eager to live forever. Members of an individual's household—servants as well as family—if persuaded to take such concoctions, were also guaranteed a prolonged life. Some individuals went to considerable trouble to achieve immortality. One man smeared his entire house with a magic potion to ensure that he would continue to live in comfort. People also tried to control their body and its functions, including breathing, in an effort to resist disease and physical decay and thereby achieve mastery over death.

Alternatively, the *fang-shih* claimed to offer introductions to those already enjoying immortality. These immortal individuals could serve as guides to others aspiring to the same state. Emperors sent expeditions to islands beyond the borders of the known world and to remote mountains, where the Immortals were believed to dwell. These beings were rumored to have supernatural powers; for example, they could become invisible or cause flowers to instantly bloom. It was said that Zhongli Quan, chief of the Immortals, could raise the dead with a mere wave of his fan.

"Nonseeking"

Apparently, the basis for belief in the Immortals was rooted in Daoist thinking. Daoist philosophy teaches that the Dao ("the Way")—understood as the wellspring of life—is limitless and therefore cannot be sought out with the human senses or reason, which are limited. The more that people try to grab hold of the Dao, the more it eludes them. Instead, if someone surrenders to the ever-changing currents of nature and life as if floating along the currents of a stream, he or she will be borne by the Dao. Daoist thinker Zhuang Zi referred to *zhenren,* or "pure beings," who, after a lifetime of "nonseeking" the Dao, had developed the ability to pass through fire without being burned and to lie down in the snow without freezing to death. Central to the philosophy of Daoism is the concept of *jang,* or "yieldedness": "As the soft yield of water cleaves obstinate stone, / So to yield with life

A Han clay lid in the form of the mountainous Isle of the Immortals. The Han believed that such a region existed, and that the beings who dwelled there had supernatural powers.

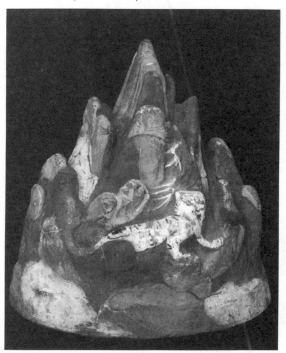

Daoism and Science

Beliefs associated with Daoism apparently stimulated scientific developments in ancient China. Based on the Daoist idea of the changeability of all things, alchemists in search of a way to turn common metals into gold observed various chemical processes. A book of alchemy from the Han period, for example, refers to mercury as "dragon" and lead as "tiger," yet at the same time it describes the chemical reaction between carbon and what is known as white lead, which produces lead metal.

Additionally, the discovery by the Chinese of magnetism appears to derive from the practice of divination. A diviner known as a geomancer was consulted in town planning to ensure that the location and direction of buildings would be in harmony with cosmic forces and would thus provide good fortune for the inhabitants. The geomancer's tools included a piece of naturally magnetic iron ore, known as lodestone, in the shape of a spoon or sometimes a fish. Acting as a rudimentary compass, the lodestone rotated on a polished board, aligning itself in a north-south direction. The familiarity of the ancient Chinese with lodestone predates 200 B.C. Evidently, the following passage, written in A.D. 83 and reproduced in Yong Yap and Arthur Cotterell's *The Early Civilization of China*, is the earliest known record of magnetism: "But when the south-controlling spoon is thrown upon the ground, it comes to rest pointing at the south."

A 16th century painting of Lao Zi, the legendary founder of Daoism.

solves the insolvable: / To yield, I have learned, is to come back again."[36]

For the ancient Chinese, Daoism was far more than a key to immortality, however. As its English translation, "the Way," implies,

Daoism was (and is) an all-encompassing approach to life. The founder of Daoism, known as Lao Zi, or "the Old Philosopher," is believed to have lived in the sixth century B.C. True to his conviction in the sustaining power of living in "yieldedness" with nature, Lao Zi eventually made his home in the wilds of China's frontier. According to the Han historian Sima Qian, before Lao Zi "retired from the world,"[37] he was persuaded to put his ideas in writing. He did so, reluctantly, in a book consisting of a mere five thousand words. This book, the *Daodejing*, begins,

> Existence is beyond the power of words
> To define . . .
> From wonder to wonder
> Existence opens.[38]

Lao Zi and his followers encouraged people to live spontaneously and without pretense, unburdened by society's rules and regulations. Daoist philosophy teaches that codes of behavior imposed by society are arbitrary and contrary to people's true nature. Cut off from their deepest selves, the Daoists believed, human beings have been kept from experiencing the full range of their abilities. In line with their antiauthoritarian views, Daoist thinkers considered governments corrupt—and corrupting. Government was therefore best kept to a minimum: "A government whose name only is known to the people"[39] was the ideal according to Daoist philosophy.

Propriety

Daoism's skepticism regarding human institutions offered the Han Chinese a counterbalance to the social conformity encouraged by Confucianism. Both philosophies spoke to people's sense of disillusionment with the spiritual practices of the time—despite the myriad government bureaus devoted to religious ceremony and display. Yet whereas Daoism spoke to the radical impulse to draw

"I, Too, Will Wag My Tail in the Mud"

For Lao Zi and many of his followers, the ideal life was that of a hermit, shunning human society and being alone in the wilderness to contemplate nature. A story about the very witty Daoist philosopher Zhuang Zi, told in Yong Yap and Arthur Cotterell's book *The Early Civilization of China*, illustrates this point.

"[A certain prince] sent two high officials to ask Zhuang Zi to take charge of the government and become chief minister. They found Zhuang Zi fishing in [the River] P'u. Intent on what he was doing he listened without turning his head. At last he said: 'I have been told there is in the capital a sacred tortoise, which has been dead for over a thousand years. And that the Prince keeps this tortoise carefully enclosed in a chest on the altar of his ancestral temple. Now would this tortoise rather be dead but considered holy, or alive and wagging its tail in the mud?' The two officials answered that it would prefer to be alive and wagging its tail in the mud. 'Clear off, then!' shouted Zhuang Zi. 'I, too, will wag my tail in the mud here.'"

from the deepest wellsprings of spiritual power, Confucianism appealed to yearnings for past traditions able—so it was believed—to create a more civil, humane world. Because Confucianism accommodated more readily to the imperial goal of an orderly, stable society, it became the dominant philosophy of the Han period—centuries after the death of Confucius himself.

The philosophy of Confucius stressed the principle of *li,* that is, "etiquette" or "propriety." In Confucius's view, the formalities of rites and rituals, social as well as religious, supported courteous and respectful dealings between people. In fact, the written character for *li* showed a sacrificial vessel containing a precious object. According to Confucius, people ought to willingly sacrifice their own desires to benefit others, thus cultivating the virtue of *jen,* or unselfishness. Discipline over wayward passions was required to maintain this sacrificial spirit: Ideally, individuals were not to lose sight of *jen* "even for the time of a single meal."[40]

Confucius taught that each person played a particular role in society—and that any ambition other than filling that role as ably as possible should be dismissed. Aspirations to play a role other than the one in which a person was cast only disrupted the order of things and led to violence. The first and foremost role one played in ancient China was that of obedient child. Confucius taught that "the root of all virtue"[41] is filial piety—that is, respect for one's parents. In Confucian thought, the family, not the individual, formed the cornerstone of society. Consequently, respect—even worship—of a person's forebears became second nature to the Chinese people.

Offerings to the Ancestors

Worship of one's ancestors, as practiced in Han China, not only expressed reverence for one's forebears but also people's yearning for prolonging life. Sacrifices of food prepared for deceased ancestors made their presence among the living a reality. Families unable to

Confucius taught the virtues of unselfishness and respect for one's parents. His philosophy greatly influenced life and thought in ancient China.

"The Tall Man"

The Chinese philosopher who perhaps most influenced the Han as well as subsequent periods was born into genteel poverty sometime around the middle of the sixth century B.C. According to legend, Confucius was born into this world with a hollow in his head—apparently, a storage place for his celebrated wisdom.

Orphaned at an early age, the young Confucius managed to get an education based on his family's links to nobility. Eventually he became one of the many roving scholars seeking positions in the courts of kings during the Warring States Period. Failing to secure a satisfactory post, he re- turned to his home state, Lu, in the northeast of China. There, he began to teach. So sterling was his reputation and so commanding his presence—he was nicknamed "the Tall Man"—that he attracted a number of disciples.

Still ambitious to influence the conduct of government, Confucius held office periodically, though invariably his high ideals clashed with the pragmatism of political realities. His last words, quoted in *The First Emperor of China,* by R. W. L. Guisso et al., lamented "The world has long strayed from the True Way."

afford an ancestral temple for performing the required sacrifices constructed an altar for this purpose in the main room of their home.

The ancient Chinese accepted the idea that the dead continued to need food and drink. In fact, the tantalizing smells of food being prepared for such ceremonies were believed to invite the spirits of ancestors back to the earth. Lost souls who failed to receive sac- rifices were believed to take revenge for their hunger pangs on the living.

To avoid such horrors and to promote continuity among the generations, celebrations devoted to ancestor worship featured a feast in which the remains of food offerings to the ancestors were shared by family members. This communal meal strengthened kinship bonds, past and present.

8 At Home

Because the duty of ancestor worship fell on male descendants, the ancient Chinese considered sons vital to the continuation of the family. A man who had only daughters feared that, at his own death, there would be no one to properly worship his ancestors. As a result, his family would come to an end. To avoid this fate, he might take a concubine, or secondary spouse. Such women came into the household without the benefit of a wedding and could not claim the status of a lawful wife. Their status was inferior to that of a man's legal wife, whom they were expected to serve. Moreover, although their sons were considered legitimate heirs to their father's name and property, such offspring remained inferior socially to the sons of the lawful wife. Although no man could have more than one wife, the number of concubines he could acquire depended on his social standing: the higher the standing, the more concubines he was allowed.

Adoption was another way for a man without a son to obtain a legal heir. However, the child adopted had to be a blood relative because only then could acceptance of his offerings by the family's ancestors be guaranteed. In Han times, a story was told about an adopted son whose offerings, because he was not related by blood, ended up being received by his own ancestors rather than those of his adopted family.

During the early Han period, most families were relatively small. The family unit generally consisted of a husband and wife—and perhaps a concubine—along with their unmarried children. Emperors, eager to weaken large and powerful families who posed a potential threat to their centralized rule, early on decreed that relatives could not live together under the same roof. By the later Han period, however, the enforcement of this restriction loosened, and large extended families became more common. Three generations—grandparents, parents, and children—might share a home, or brothers might move in together and raise a family that included aunts, uncles, nephews, nieces, and cousins.

A boy, then, might live his entire life under one roof, but when a young woman married, she left her own family and became part of her husband's. Keeping them financially dependent, young women were prohibited from inheriting property which all went to their brothers. A girl's dowry, which was slight compared with what male siblings could expect from their inheritance, amounted to the only share she had in her family's property—and even that went to her husband's family when she married.

The Critical Matter of Arranged Marriages

Because descent followed the male line, a daughter was considered a liability to her family. Thus, girls were married off as soon as possible in ancient China. Pan Chao, the sister of historian Pan Ku and a scholar herself, wrote that she "took up the dustpan and broom"[42]—

A painting depicts a concubine (right) playing an instrument for her lover. A man's social standing determined the number of concubines he was allowed.

that is, became a wife—at the age of fourteen. Generally, women in Han China were married between the ages of thirteen and sixteen. The average man, meanwhile, married when he was anywhere from sixteen to thirty years old. Personal preferences were irrelevant when it came to choosing a marriage partner. The purpose of marriage was to produce offspring and continue the family line. Such a critical matter was best left outside the whims of desire. Marriages were instead arranged in a businesslike fashion by the parents of the future bride and groom through a go-between. The go-between, usually a friend or relative, handled all of the preliminaries up to the betrothal, or engagement, at which time all details, such as the amount of the bridal dowry, were settled. The go-between, for example, reported the results of divination to determine the favorability of a union.

When the wedding day arrived, the bride's parents advised her, "Be respectful and courteous, do not disobey your husband."[43] Just as she had been obedient to her father as a daughter, she must be subservient to her husband. In public at least, a dutiful wife never addressed her husband directly by name. In addition, she handed him objects on a tray rather than by hand to avoid breaching custom by touching him.

On her way to her new home, the bride was expected to cry tears of sorrow over leaving her family as well as tears of joy over the prospect of joining her husband's household. Before the groom properly received his bride, his father instructed him: "Go to welcome your helpmate in order to fulfill our affairs in the ancestral temple."[44] On the very next day after the wedding, the husband introduced his new wife to his ancestors at the family shrine. Not until she assumed her role in the worship of her husband's ancestors was a woman considered a lawful wife. Until that time, she

could be sent back to her family—the horses and cart that had brought her were kept at the groom's home, ready to return her if need be.

Grounds for Divorce

Although a wife's status was more secure than a concubine's, she still faced the possibility of being ousted from her husband's home. A husband could divorce his wife on seven grounds. These included disobedience to her parents-in-law, infertility, adultery, theft, incurable disease, jealousy, and talkativeness. Offenses seen as justifying a divorce were numerous and sometimes trivial. For example, one man divorced his wife for not fetching water quickly enough to give to his thirsty mother.

Serious concerns of the ancient Chinese underlay these grounds for divorce. Infertility

---

An Eligible Bachelor

A number of considerations went into determining a suitable marriage partner, from wealth and potential for advancement to the number of times that someone had been widowed—it was believed that the premature death of a husband or wife could be traced to the "unlucky" character of a spouse. The following story from Pan Ku's history of the Han, published in T'ung-tsu Ch'u's *Han Social Structure,* reflects such considerations.

"When Ch'en P'ing grew up and became of marriageable age, no one among the rich was willing to give him [his daughter to marry]. P'ing also was ashamed [to marry] a poor one.
    Chang Fu's granddaughter had been married five times, and her husbands had all

died. There was no one who dared to marry her, but P'ing desired to have her. . . .
    When Chang Fu saw him at a funeral, he . . . admired P'ing . . . and followed him to his house. His house was in a poor lane . . . and had a worn-out straw mat for a door. But outside the door there were many ruts from the carriages of prominent people.
    When Chang Fu returned home, he addressed his son, Chung, saying, 'I wish to give my granddaughter to Ch'en P'ing. . . . Can such a handsome man as Ch'en P'ing be poor and low permanently?' Finally he gave the girl [to P'ing]. Because P'ing was poor, he lent him the gifts for the betrothal, and gave him money for the wine and meat for the wedding feast."

could bring on divorce since the family's survival was at stake—in ancient China, the woman was generally blamed for lack of offspring. Similarly, a woman who committed adultery might bear another man's son; such a son's offering would benefit that man's ancestors, not her husband's. A woman's chronic illness, meanwhile, prohibited her from preparing the sacrificial offering to her husband's ancestors, making her an unfit wife. Displays of jealousy and talkativeness, believed to spread gossip, were not tolerated because they stirred up discord in the household.

A wife did have some protection against being arbitrarily divorced and sent away, however. A man was denied a divorce under three conditions. First, a husband must stay married to his wife if she mourned the death of one of his parents for three years. This condition reinforced the notion that the relationship that a woman had with her in-laws was more important than her relationship with her husband. Second, if a wife had no relatives who might take her in, her husband could not turn her out. Finally, if a man had acquired wealth since their marriage, he was prevented from divorcing his wife.

Although a woman was afforded these rudimentary protections, her options remained limited if she were dissatisfied with her marriage. No grounds existed, at least officially, for a woman to divorce her husband in Han times.

Father Knows Best

In ancient China, men had almost complete control over their families. Even as adults, sons might be beaten by their fathers. Moreover, strictness on the part of parents was expected. "Ten Hsün, although broadminded and tolerant of others, was very severe to his

family," an account from Han times reads. "When his sons came to call upon him, he never gave them a seat or received them with a mild countenance."[45]

Not surprisingly, in Chinese families the fathers named the children. Three months after birth, when considered fit to be in his presence, a child was brought to his or her father to receive a *ming,* or personal name. This the father spoke in a childish voice so as not to

A ceramic male figure from the Han dynasty. Men in ancient China enjoyed far more rights and a higher status in society than women.

Divorce

Divorce remained an option for Han-era couples. The reasons that one man gives for divorcing his wife are spelled out in a letter to the woman's brother, published in *Chinese Civilization and Society: A Sourcebook*, edited by Patricia Buckley Ebrey.

"Since antiquity it has always been considered a great disaster to have one's household be dominated by a woman. Now this disaster has befallen me. If I eat too much or too little or if I drink too much or too little, she jumps all over me. . . . She glowers with her eyes and clenches her fists tightly in anger over things which are purely the product of her imagination.

Food and clothing are scattered all over the house. Winter clothes which have become frayed are not patched. Even though the rest of us are very careful to be neat, she turns the house into a mess.

When the respectable members of our family try to reason with her, she flings insults at them and makes sharp retorts. She never regrets her scandalous behavior and never allows her heart to be moved."

frighten the infant. Although the number of surnames, or family names, in Han China was relatively limited, fathers could choose from a wide selection of personal names for a son or daughter. This name could express a wish or prayer, including the desire for a lengthy life. In the periodic government population registers, the personal, or given, name was usually written after the surname.

To demonstrate the deference that children owed their father, a number of restrictions governed their behavior when in his presence. Children were forbidden, for example, to lean or rest against anything, spit, or blow their noses when in the same room with him. Such behavior was considered disrespectful.

School Days

Within the family, Chinese children learned the formalities of behavior that would be of utmost importance to their functioning in society. Children of the *nong* also were trained in work around the farm since they had duties to perform even at a young age. Boys from wealthy families, who were not expected to work, received instruction in the basics of writing, archery, music, and the performance of rituals, which would prepare them for entering their local district school at the age of ten.

While their sisters stayed at home learning such domestic arts as unwinding silk cocoons and preparing food offerings for the ancestors, sons of the middle and upper classes spent their time in school. Education in Han China aimed to build character as well as to develop skills and talents. Students were drilled in lessons in history, ritual, morality, and politics from the classic Confucian texts. They were also instructed in what were called the six sciences: dancing, music, archery, chariot driving, writing, and arithmetic. To assist in teaching the reading and writing of the complex pictograms making up the Chinese written language, teachers assembled vocabulary lists. These lists grouped together characters for objects of the same category—for example, *house, hut,* and *hall.*

The school curriculum depended on the season. In spring and summer, archery practice and other outdoor exercises were the focus. In fall and winter, however, lessons revolved around indoor studies such as writing.

Schools in ancient China were enclaves of male adolescents. Women were barred from them altogether, and other than teachers,

A Han sculpture of a mounted archer. Archery was one of the "six sciences" taught to boys in Han schools.

male adults were allowed entrance only for special ceremonies. The schools themselves were located outside the bounds of a town or village, and a semicircular ditch around the school building physically separated it from the outside world.

Hats and Hairpins

When young men of the upper classes completed their schooling, at about the age of twenty, they returned home and prepared themselves for the ritual marking their entrance into adult life. Known as the capping ceremony, this initiation rite was held on a day determined favorable by divination. Friends and relatives gathered for the celebration in the home of the young man's family.

The ceremony itself involved changing the hairstyle worn throughout childhood—two "horns" on each side of the head—into the style associated with men in the culture: a bun or coil atop the head. Then a sequence of hats were placed on the initiate's head. First, a plain cloth cap, or *kuan,* indicated that he was now grown to adulthood and would no longer bare his head in public. The attendant priest pronounced, "In this happy month, on this lucky day, for the first time the hat is placed on your head. Banish all childish thoughts; you must now behave in conformity with the Virtue of a perfect man. May your old age be happy and your fortune ever increase in splendour!"[46] The young man then, in turn, received two additional ceremonial hats: one representing his readiness to go to battle for his people and the other to lead rituals honoring his ancestors—

The Value of Education

The ancient Chinese prized education as a means for young men to better their lives. The value of young men applying themselves diligently to their studies is suggested in the following excerpt about the Confucian philosopher Mencius and is found in *Chinese Civilization and Society: A Sourcebook,* edited by Patricia Buckley Ebrey:

"When Mencius was young, he came home from school one day and found his mother was weaving at the loom. She asked him, 'Is school out already?'

He replied, 'I left because I felt like it.'

His mother took her knife and cut the finished cloth on her loom. Mencius was startled and asked why. She replied, 'Your neglecting your studies is very much like my cutting the cloth. The superior person studies to establish a reputation and gather wide knowledge. . . . If you do not study now, you will surely end up as a menial servant and will never be free from troubles.'"

both signaling his being born to a new life. From now on, the young man was entitled to all of the privileges and duties of an adult male of his class. He could now put on the armor of a warrior, conduct ancestral worship, accept an official post—after passing qualifying exams, of course—and take a wife.

Once a girl reached marriageable age, she underwent a similar, if less elaborate, ceremony to mark her initiation into adulthood. Instead of a series of caps, she received a hairpin allowing her to arrange her hair atop her head in a more adult style; as a child, she had been limited to braiding her hair into a cross in the middle.

Signaling their emergence into a new phase in their lives, both boys and girls received a new name at their respective initiations. This name, or *tzu,* replaced their childhood name, or *ming.* They could then be properly addressed in public without revealing their personal name. This granting of a new name, which secured for them a sense of privacy, was a gesture of respect that, as adults, they were now entitled. In addition, a man might be given a secondary name later in life, usually alluding to some event in which he played a part.

A statuette of a Han warrior. Donning the armor of a warrior was one of the many privileges young men of the upper class in Han China earned when they became adults.

Hun and P'o

The multiplicity of names that a person bore throughout life helped signify the role that he or she played in China's highly stratified society. That role continued into the afterlife, and notable people might even receive an additional name or title following their death. The ancient Chinese conceived of dying as a separation of the two distinct souls that they believed came together in the living person. Death released these souls, known as the *hun* and the *p'o*, to pursue their different destinies.

The *hun* was believed on occasion to leave the living body and wander about on its own, which was the way the ancient Chinese explained dreams. This departure, however, was only temporary. After death, the *hun* quit the body for good, headed for Shangdi's heavenly home. The journey was not an easy one. Along the way the *hun* had to fend off monsters bent on devouring it. It also had to provide the proper password to each gatekeeper of heaven's nine levels. Such a difficult transit, with its series of trials, required a guide. The priest who recited the prayers before and after a person's burial served this purpose. So did shamans who claimed to be capable of traveling the heavens and so could show the *hun* how to proceed safely.

The *p'o*, meanwhile, remained with the buried or entombed body. There it lived on the offerings provided by the descendants of the deceased. An underworld dwelling was imagined for the *p'o*, a kind of counterpart for the heavenly home of the *hun*. Known as the Yellow Springs, or Nine Springs, this realm was ruled by Keui-wang, the king of the ghosts, in the same way heaven was presided over by Shangdi. In both places, souls could meet and resume a familiar existence. Social ranking continued to be observed as on the earth, with wives remaining subordinate to their husbands and children to their parents.

The Funeral

In consideration of the *p'o*, efforts were made to preserve the dead person's body as long as possible. Small pieces of jade were occasionally placed over the eyes and under the tongue, as jade supposedly prevented the body's decay. Sometimes efforts to prevent decay were taken to extremes. A suit constructed of nearly twenty-five hundred jade pieces knit together with gold wire totally encased the dead body of Prince Liu Sheng, for instance.

Care was taken to groom the bodies of the dead so they could enter their new existence looking their best. Before burial, the body and hair of the deceased were ceremonially washed. In addition, their fingernails and toenails were clipped. In the coffin, along with the corpse, lay small cloth bags containing cuttings of the person's nails and hair. These parings were collected throughout life so the deceased might go complete into the next world.

How quickly people were buried in ancient China depended on their station in life. Commoners of limited means were laid in the ground right away. The body of a wealthy, influential person, however, might be on display for a couple of days before burial. During this time, the family received visitors expressing their condolences; likewise, relatives took turns day and night in mournful crying.

These lamentations continued during the burial procession. To support them in their grief as they walked along, mourners carried staves. Leading the procession, a shaman shook a halberd in each of the four directions—north, south, east, and west—to keep evil influences off the road. The coffin followed on a cart draped with strands of red and black silk.

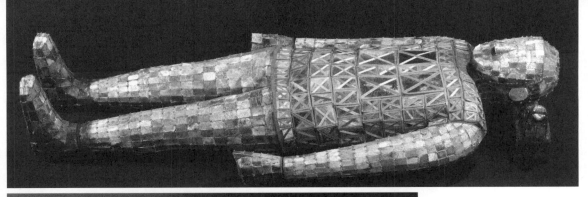

The ancient Chinese took great care to ensure that the deceased would remain well-preserved and comfortable in the afterlife. (Above) the jade burial suit of a Han princess. (Left) an elaborately decorated, lacquered coffin from a Han tomb.

A Pit or a Mound?

Finally, the procession halted at the burial site. The wide disparity among the rich and poor in ancient China continued in their options for a final resting place. The poverty-stricken might not even have the benefit of a coffin, their bodies wrapped only in some matting before being laid in a pit. The rich, by contrast, could anticipate a brick or stone vault along with a wooden coffin protecting their corpse. The coffin's wood planks were often decorated with paint and were sometimes lacquered.

During the Han dynasty, the custom developed of piling earth over a tomb as a kind of landmark or monument; such mounds might rise to a height of ten feet. Still, the main way that people displayed their wealth and prestige was to build themselves an elaborate tomb prior to their death, complete with towers and stone beasts guarding the entrance. Such structures were honeycombed with chambers and passageways connecting a series of shrines. Scenes from familiar moral tales were often painted on the walls. Other wall paintings might remind the deceased of joyous times in their lives, such as sumptuous banquets or lively entertainments with dancers and musicians.

To ensure comfort for the deceased in their next phase of life, a number of material goods accompanied the burial of corpses. Along with silver robe hooks, lacquer bowls, and bronze lampstands, clay models of homes and even entire estates, including granaries and pig pens, were frequently sealed up in tombs. Clay figures representing servants, dressed like dolls in miniature pieces of clothing, stood ready to spring to life at their master's call. Death, the ancient Chinese were convinced, brought no end to one's prescribed role in life.

Epilogue

A New Outlook

After a long dominance, marked by political as well as cultural expansion, the Han dynasty collapsed in the third century A.D. Large landholding families scrambled to fill the power vacuum created by the imperial government's decline, thus plunging China into three hundred years of warfare. Nomadic tribes set up their own dynasties in the northern part of the empire, ruling over a humiliated Chinese population. Having settled into a life of relative stability and increasing productivity under the Han, the people of China now struggled through a period of chaos.

The rule of the Sui dynasty, beginning in 589, reunited China. The brief Sui regime was marked by a flurry of public-works projects aimed at rebuilding China's roads and waterways, which were devastated by years of warfare. The *nong* barely had a chance to recuperate from the ravages of war before being conscripted to labor on these projects, which included the construction of a canal system linking China's northern and southern regions. Such improvements to the infrastructure led to commercial expansion, which in turn led to social change in the subsequent dynasty, the Tang.

Consolidating China's reunification, the Tang dynasty (618–907) strengthened the central government, elaborating administrative codes and penal laws and refining the system of civil service examinations initiated in the Han era. At the same time, Tang rulers promoted educational policies that equipped increasing numbers of talented young men for government service. Rebellion and invasion had already weakened the grip of the old aristocracy on the privileges of government office. During the Tang era, individual talent became progressively more important than blood ties in acquiring government posts. As class barriers began to break down, increasing social mobility even for the *shang*, a new commercial economy took hold.

A New Worldview

The emphasis on commerce broke down cultural as well as social barriers. China was more open to foreign influence than ever before. Popular taste changed, elevating the exotic over the traditional. Emblematic of this change, traditional art forms gave way to styles and motifs imported from the Greek, or Hellenistic, world, so that, for example, Hellenistic bunches of grapes began to appear on Tang bronze mirrors. A more cosmopolitan worldview had successfully overtaken a simpler, more provincial outlook; although the ancient world that had produced this outlook would continue to be honored in Chinese thought and writing, its reality had vanished.

The Tang capital, a rebuilt Changan, flourished as an international center. Along with exotic new products, the capital's many foreign inhabitants brought with them new ideas. Helping to transmit these ideas was the new technology of woodcut printing. The invention of printing during the Tang period led

A Sui dynasty cave painting of a seated Buddha and bodhisattavas. The Buddhist religion, which was introduced during the Han dynasty, later took hold in China and would have a long-lasting impact on Chinese life.

to the stirrings of an information revolution in China. The era's proliferation of poets notwithstanding, it was Buddhist zealots eager to spread their teachings who produced some of China's first printed pages, including written charms and devotional books.

Buddhism had a more lasting and profound impact on Chinese life than any other early import. Introduced into China during Han times, the Buddhist religion found a receptive audience in a population dislocated by war and upheaval following the end of the Han dynasty. Buddhism's promise of release from suffering appealed to all social classes, from disillusioned intellectuals to peasants yearning for a source of infinite solace. The new spiritual outlook that Buddhism provided was embraced and at the same time transformed by the Chinese people. In Chinese Buddhism, godlike, compassionate beings known as bodhisattvas protected humans from ghosts and guided the faithful in the spiritual practices required by the new religion.

The bodhisattavas assumed much of the guardianship role of ancestors for the Chinese people, loosening ties to traditional Confucian practice without breaking them altogether. In fact, Confucianism peacefully coexisted with the growing appeal of the new faith. Indeed, the continuity of family and bureaucratic institutions helped maintain a familiar order to the Chinese way of life, at least until the upheavals of the Maoist revolution over a thousand years later. Nevertheless, the changes the nation underwent following the Han dynasty can legitimately be seen as ending the chronicle of ancient China.

Notes

Introduction: A Balancing Act

1. Yong Yap and Arthur Cotterell, *The Early Civilization of China*. New York: G. P. Putnam's Sons, 1975, p. 41.
2. R. W. L. Guisso et al., *The First Emperor of China*. New York: Carol, 1989, p. 14.
3. Guisso, *The First Emperor of China*, p. 200.

Chapter 1: On the Land

4. Quoted in Cho-yun Hsu, *Han Agriculture: The Formation of Early Chinese Agrarian Economy (206 B.C.–A.D. 220)*. Seattle: University of Washington Press, 1980, p. 170.
5. Quoted in Hsu, *Han Agriculture*, p. 162.
6. Quoted in T'ung-tsu Ch'u, *Han Social Structure*. Seattle: University of Washington Press, 1972, p. 110.
7. Quoted in Hsu, *Han Agriculture*, p. 130.
8. Quoted in Hsu, *Han Agriculture*, pp. 244–45.
9. Quoted in Ch'u, *Han Social Structure*, p. 110.
10. Michael Loewe, *Everyday Life in Early Imperial China: During the Han Period, 202 B.C.–A.D. 220*. London: Carousel Books, 1973, pp. 178–79.

Chapter 2: In the City

11. Quoted in Raymond Dawson, *The Chinese Experience*. London: Weidenfeld and Nicolson, 1978, p. 59.
12. Quoted in Loewe, *Everyday Life in Early Imperial China*, p. 131.
13. Quoted in Loewe, *Everyday Life in Early Imperial China*, p. 136.
14. Quoted in Kwang-chih Chang, *Early Chinese Civilization: Anthropological Perspectives*. Cambridge, MA: Harvard University Press, 1976, p. 126.
15. Quoted in Chang, *Early Chinese Civilization*, pp. 46–47.
16. Quoted in Wang Zhongshu, *Han Civilization*, trans. K. C. Chang et al. New Haven, CT: Yale University Press, 1982, p. 5.

Chapter 3: In Power

17. Quoted in Yap and Cotterell, *The Early Civilization of China*, p. 81.
18. Burton Watson, ed. and trans., *Courtier and Commoner in Ancient China: Selections from the "History of the Former Han" by Pan Ku*. New York: Columbia University Press, 1974, pp. 259–60.
19. Quoted in Ch'u, *Han Social Structure*, p. 365.

Chapter 4: At War

20. Watson, *Courtier and Commoner in Ancient China*, p. 15.
21. Loewe, *Everyday Life in Early Imperial China*, p. 191.
22. Loewe, *Everyday Life in Early Imperial China*, pp. 80–81.
23. Quoted in Guisso, *The First Emperor of China*, p. 146.
24. Quoted in Guisso, *The First Emperor of China*, p. 150.

Chapter 5: In Business

25. Quoted in Irene M. Franck and David M. Brownstone, *The Silk Road: A History*. New York: Facts On File, 1986, p. 12.

26. Quoted in Zhongshu, *Han Civilization,* p. 107.
27. Quoted in Ch'u, *Han Social Structure,* p. 121.
28. Quoted in Ch'u, *Han Social Structure,* p. 340.
29. Quoted in Loewe, *Everyday Life in Early Imperial China,* p. 184.

Chapter 6: With Artistry

30. Quoted in Dawson, *The Chinese Experience,* p. 229.
31. Quoted in Yap and Cotterell, *The Early Civilization of China,* p. 22.
32. Quoted in Loewe, *Everyday Life in Early Imperial China,* p. 100.
33. Quoted in Dawson, *The Chinese Experience,* p. 240.

Chapter 7: In Harmony

34. Quoted in Loewe, *Everyday Life in Early Imperial China,* p. 105.
35. Edward H. Schafer and the Editors of Time-Life Books, *Ancient China.* New York: Time-Life Books, 1967, p. 103.
36. Quoted in Yap and Cotterell, *The Early Civilization of China,* p. 60.

37. Quoted in Yap and Cotterell, *The Early Civilization of China,* p. 59.
38. Quoted in Yap and Cotterell, *The Early Civilization of China,* p. 59.
39. Quoted in Guisso, *The First Emperor of China,* p. 104.
40. Quoted in Henri Maspero, *China in Antiquity,* trans. Frank A. Kierman Jr. Amherst: University of Massachusetts Press, 1978, p. 291.
41. Quoted in Guisso, *The First Emperor of China,* p. 99.

Chapter 8: At Home

42. Quoted in Ch'u, *Han Social Structure,* pp. 298–99.
43. Quoted in Ch'u, *Han Social Structure,* p. 50.
44. Quoted in Ch'u, *Han Social Structure,* p. 34.
45. Quoted in Ch'u, *Han Social Structure,* p. 300.
46. Quoted in Maspero, *China in Antiquity,* p. 80.

Glossary

acupuncture: A traditional Chinese medical practice in which needles are inserted at critical points in the body to treat illness or relieve pain.

bureaucracy: A system of government in which duties are specialized, workers are ranked, and paperwork seems to multiply.

cast: To reshape a material, such as a metal, by pouring it in liquid form into a mold until it hardens.

civil service: The group of workers who manage and carry out the policies of government; they must pass a test for employment.

concubine: A secondary spouse, who has less status than a legal wife.

conscript: A person forced to do labor or serve in the army.

divination: The art or practice of trying to determine what the future will bring, often by interpreting signs and omens.

dowry: The money or property that a bride brings with her into marriage.

edict: A government proclamation that carries the force of law.

gong: The group of people in ancient Chinese society who worked as artisans and technicians.

halberd: An axlike weapon mounted on a pole.

hsien-ch'ing: Meaning "previous request," a privilege enjoyed by officials in imperial China whereby they could only be arrested with the emperor's approval.

huangdi: The title given to China's emperor, acknowledging his supreme power.

hun: The soul believed to leave the body and travel to heaven when a person dies.

kuan: The plain cap worn in public by Chinese men.

lacquer: A hard, glossy coating that can be decorated with paint or inlaid material.

li: In Confucian philosophy, the principle of "propriety," or proper behavior; also a measurement of distance.

millet: A kind of grass that produces a grain for food.

mortar and pestle: A sturdy bowl and club-shaped tool for pounding and pulverizing material.

mou: A Chinese unit of land measurement, equal to about one-sixth of an acre.

nong: The group of people in ancient Chinese society who worked the fields.

nu: The group of people in ancient Chinese society who served as slaves.

pavilion: A building in a park or other place of recreation that provides shelter as well as decoration.

phoenix: A mythical bird thought by the ancient Chinese to bring prosperity; according to myth, at the end of its long life it set its nest on fire and then rises from the ashes, once again young.

pictogram: A picture used to represent a word.

p'o: The soul believed to remain with the body and to continue to require food.

qin: A musical instrument whose strings are plucked by hand, much like a lute.

shaman: A religious leader claiming magical powers.

shang: The group of people in ancient Chinese society who worked in commerce and trade.

sheng: A musical instrument made of bamboo pipes.

tenant farmer: Someone who farms land owned by another and pays rent, usually in a portion of the crops grown.

tai-tien: A method for planting seeds into shallow furrows rather than scattering them randomly; a more efficient way of sowing developed in Han China.

t'ien-ming: Meaning "mandate of heaven," the ancient Chinese principle that the right to rule depends on the approval of divine forces.

t'ien tzu: The title "son of heaven," claiming near-divine authority for the ruler of China.

ward: A section of a city walled off from other sections.

wu: People in ancient China serving as shamans.

Xiangnu: The people living north of China, beyond the Great Wall.

yang: In Chinese thought, the universal force or energy representing light, heat, and dryness; combined with yin, it produces all that exists.

yin: In Chinese thought, the universal force or energy representing darkness, cold, and wetness; combined with yang, it produces all that exists.

For Further Reading

Arthur Cotterell, *Ancient China*. New York: Knopf, 1994. Much detail is compactly presented in this overview of ancient Chinese culture. It is organized thematically, has numerous color illustrations, and many photographs of artifacts.

Penelope Hughes-Stanton, *See Inside an Ancient Chinese Town*. Rev. ed. New York: Warwick, 1986. Various aspects of life during the latter part of the Han dynasty are glimpsed as the reader is taken on a brief tour of Loyang, the second of the Han's capital cities. Includes a glossary and a time line comparing happenings in ancient China with those around the world.

Caroline Lazo, *The Terra Cotta Army of Emperor Qin*. New York: New Discovery Books, 1993. Abounds in illuminating details about the army of clay warriors guarding the emperor's tomb and sheds light on military matters in early imperial China. The author's examination is balanced, and her writing is lively and absorbing. Amply illustrated.

Hazel Mary Martel, *The Ancient Chinese*. New York: New Discovery Books, 1993. Surveys ancient China's history and people in less than a hundred pages. Plentiful illustrations enliven the book's straightforward, topical presentation. Includes a glossary.

Tim McNeese, *The Great Wall of China*. San Diego: Lucent Books, 1997. Chronicles the entire history of the Great Wall, from its inception to its restoration beginning in the 1980s. Explores the ancient Chinese tradition of wall building before detailing the engineering feat itself. Black-and-white illustrations throughout.

Suzanne Williams, *Made in China: Ideas and Inventions from Ancient China*. Berkeley, CA: Pacific View, 1996. Reviews ideas and technology affecting life in ancient China. Brief thematic sections cover, for example, silk production and trade. Lots of color illustrations.

Works Consulted

Kwang-chih Chang, *Early Chinese Civilization: Anthropological Perspectives*. Cambridge, MA: Harvard University Press, 1976. A scholarly reconstruction of the Shang and Zhou cultures, forming a background to the Han period. Topics range from food preparation to mythology. Technical.

T'ung-tsu Ch'u, *Han Social Structure*. Seattle: University of Washington Press, 1972. An in-depth study of Han society. Includes a chapter devoted to the position of women. Nearly half the book reproduces primary sources.

Raymond Dawson, *The Chinese Experience*. London: Weidenfeld and Nicolson, 1978. A fairly readable survey of China's culture and society from early to modern times. This overview not only provides insights into the evolution of the Chinese civilization but also reveals its most constant features, such as Confucianism and a bureaucratic government system.

Patricia Buckley Ebrey, *Chinese Civilization and Society: A Sourcebook*. New York: Free Press, 1981. A compilation of primary source material exploring Chinese culture and arranged chronologically. Brief introductions provide historical context. Helpful reference information is provided, including explanations of weights, measures, and currency.

Irene M. Franck and David M. Brownstone, *The Silk Road: A History*. New York: Facts On File, 1986. A comprehensive history of the amalgam of trade routes that first linked China with the Mediterranean world. The Han period plays significantly in that history as marking, according to tradition, the opening of the Silk Road. Illustrated with maps and black-and-white drawings and photos.

R. W. L. Guisso et al., *The First Emperor of China*. New York: Carol, 1989. A companion book to a Canadian-produced film documentary on China's first emperor. The authors attempt to balance negative views of the emperor by portraying him as an energetic, forward-thinking ruler. Abundantly illustrated and engrossing throughout.

Cho-yun Hsu, *Han Agriculture: The Formation of Early Chinese Agrarian Economy (206 B.C.–A.D. 220)*. Seattle: University of Washington Press, 1980. A thorough examination of agricultural policy and practice during the Han dynasty. Much attention is given to archaeological evidence and primary source material. It is often technical, but summaries are provided throughout.

Evelyn Lip, *Feng Shui: Environments of Power, a Study of Chinese Architecture*. London: Academy Group, 1995. While the author mostly reviews structures built after the Han, she does discuss general characteristics of traditional architecture and landscaping, including their metaphysical significance. Illustrations as well as a glossary are provided.

Michael Loewe, *Everyday Life in Early Imperial China: During the Han Period, 202 B.C.–A.D. 220*. London: Carousel Books, 1973. A compact study of life during the

Han dynasty. Geared to the general reader rather than the scholar, the text is far from dry. Some black-and-white illustrations.

Henri Maspero, *China in Antiquity*, trans. Frank A. Kierman Jr. Amherst: University of Massachusetts Press, 1978. Drawing on classical texts—such as the *Book of History* and the *Book of Poetry*, edited during the Han—the author portrays life in feudal China and many of the customs that continued in rural areas into the Han. Contains plenty of detail: Some of it is tedious, but much of it is fascinating.

Edward H. Schafer and the Editors of Time-Life Books, *Ancient China*. New York: Time-Life Books, 1967. A thematic survey extending into the Tang dynasty. Generously illustrated with picture essays. Lively writing.

N. Diane Smith, *Sun Tzu: "The Art of War."* Bethesda, MD: Discovery Communications, 1994. A documentary introducing the viewer to *The Art of War* and its influence on both Western and Eastern worlds. Includes an analysis of the Vietnam War from the perspective of Sun Zi's (Sun Tzu's) philosophy of wresting victory from conflict.

Burton Watson, ed. and trans., *Courtier and Commoner in Ancient China: Selections from the "History of the Former Han" by Pan Ku*. New York: Columbia University Press, 1974. A translation of ten chapters from the biography section of this first-century A.D. forerunner of dynastic histories. Explanatory notes are provided. The introduction describes the evolution of history writing in ancient China.

Yong Yap and Arthur Cotterell, *The Early Civilization of China*. New York: G. P. Putnam's Sons, 1975. A fairly comprehensive overview of the period. The authors present a lot of information in a readable, accessible way. Illustrated.

Wang Zhongshu, *Han Civilization*. Trans. K. C. Chang et al. New Haven, CT: Yale University Press, 1982. This book summarizes archaeological evidence pertaining to the material culture of the Han period, including tools, utensils, and artifacts. Based on lectures given by the author, one of China's principle archaeologists, the text mostly avoids being too technical. Contains plenty of black-and-white photographs of archaeological finds.

Index

Picture Credits

Cover photo: Philadelphia Free Library/Giraudon, Paris/SuperStock

Archive Photos, 78

©Asian Art & Archaeology, Inc./Corbis, 25, 29, 58, 63, 66, 67, 74, 76, 90, 95 (top and bottom)

©Bettmann/Corbis, 14, 15, 17, 27, 31, 41

©The Bowers Museum of Cultural Art/ Corbis, 82

©Burstein Collection/Corbis, 45

©Pierre Colombel/Corbis, 42, 97

Corbis, 69

Corbis-Bettmann, 80

Denman Waldo Ross Collection, Courtesy Museum of Fine Arts, Boston, 37

©Ric Ergenbright/Corbis, 56

Giraudon/Art Resource, 23

©Wolfgang Kaehler/Corbis, 51

©Charles and Josette Lenars/Corbis, 61, 93

Library of Congress, 85

©Kevin R. Morris/Corbis, 8, 59

©Royal Ontario Museum/Brian Boyle/Corbis, 22, 64, 92

©Royal Ontario Museum/Bill Robertson/ Corbis, 35

©Royal Ontario Museum/Richard Swiecki, 65

©Joseph Sohm, ChromoSohm, Inc./ Corbis, 52

Stock Montage, Inc., 44, 47

©Keren Su/Corbis, 21

the**art**archive/Bibliotheque Nationale, Paris, 10, 38

the**art**archive/British Library, 32

the**art**archive/British Museum, 83, 88

the**art**archive/Freer Gallery of Art, 11, 12, 72

the**art**archive/Victoria and Albert Museum, 19

Baldwin H. Ward/Corbis-Bettman, 24

About the Author

Amy Allison has traveled through much of Asia, including Japan, Hong Kong, and Thailand. Asian culture is a focus of interest for Allison, who lives in the Los Angeles area along with her husband, Dave Edison. Allison has contributed poetry to *Cricket* magazine and is the author of *Building History: Shakespeare's Globe,* also published by Lucent Books.